SOUS VIDE

The Complete Cookbook! Best Sous Vide Recipes for Everyone Made Simple

John Peters

© **Copyright 2020 - All rights reserved.**

The content contained within this book may not be reproduced, duplicated or transmitted without direct written permission from the author or the publisher.

Under no circumstances will any blame or legal responsibility be held against the publisher, or author, for any damages, reparation, or monetary loss due to the information contained within this book, either directly or indirectly.

Legal Notice:

This book is copyright protected. It is only for personal use. You cannot amend, distribute, sell, use, quote or paraphrase any part, or the content within this book, without the consent of the author or publisher.

Disclaimer Notice:

Please note the information contained within this document is for educational and entertainment purposes only. All effort has been executed to present accurate, up to date, reliable, complete information. No warranties of any kind are declared or implied. Readers acknowledge that the author is not engaged in the rendering of legal, financial, medical or professional advice. The content within this book has been derived from various sources. Please consult a licensed professional before attempting any techniques outlined in this book.

By reading this document, the reader agrees that under no circumstances is the author responsible for any losses, direct or indirect, that are incurred as a result of the use of the information contained within this document, including, but not limited to, errors, omissions, or inaccuracies.

TABLE OF CONTENTS

Introduction 1

Chapter One: An Introduction To Sous Vide 2
    What Is Sous Vide? 2
    How Does It Work? 2
    Where Does Sous Vide Come From? 3
    Why Use Sous Vide? 4
        Consistency 4
        Delicious Food 4
        Improves Quality 4
        Better Nutrition 4
        Avoid Under Or Overcooking 4
        Easy Meals 5
        Large Quantities 5

Chapter Two: What Do You Need For Sous Vide? 6
    Different Sous Vide Machines 6
    Immersion Circulator 6
    Sous Vide Water Oven 6
    Sous Vide Packaging 7
    How To Use Sous Vide? 7
    Temperature For Different Meats 9
        Ribeye, Porterhouse, And Strip Steaks 9
        Hamburgers 10
        Tenderloin Steaks 11
        Chicken Breasts 12
        Chicken Thighs 13
        Pork Chops And Roast 13
        Tough Cuts Of Pork 14
        Pork Ribs 14
        Fish 15
        Vegetables 15
        Fruits 16

Chapter Three: Sous Vide Pickle Recipes 17
    Pickled Vegetables 17
    Pickled Spring Onions 19
    Pickled Asparagus With Lemon 20
    Pickled Kumquats 21
    Spicy Pickled Pineapple 22

Chapter Four: Sous Vide Jams And Preserves 23
    Bourbon-Maple Chutney 23
    Blueberry Compote 25
    Spicy Rhubarb Compote 26

Sous Vide Strawberry-Rhubarb Jam ... 27
Sous Vide Peaches ... 28
Raspberry Preserves ... 29
Strawberry-Basil Maple Syrup ... 30

Chapter Five: Sous Vide Sauces ... 31

Cranberry Sauce ... 31
Tomato Basil Pasta Sauce ... 32
Béarnaise Sauce ... 33
Tomato Sauce ... 34

Chapter Six: Sous Vide Infusions, Canning Beans And Grains ... 35

Infused Olive Oil ... 35
Infused Vinegar ... 36
Grains In Canning Jars ... 37
Sous Vide Navy Beans, With Prior Soaking ... 38
Sous Vide Beans, Without Soaking ... 39
Lentils In Canning Jars ... 40

Chapter Seven: Sous Vide Beverage Recipes ... 41

Spiked Hot Chocolate ... 41
Ponche Crema ... 43
Sous Vide 'Cold' Brew Coffee ... 43
Limoncello ... 45
Eggnog ... 46
Jalapeño Vodka ... 46
Pear Shrub ... 48
Raspberry Cordial ... 49
Sorrel Punch (Jamaican Christmas Punch) ... 50

Chapter Eight: Breakfast Recipes ... 51

Overnight Oatmeal ... 51
Overnight Oatmeal With Stewed Fruit Compote ... 52
French Toast ... 53
Perfect Egg Tostada ... 54
Poached Eggs In Hash Brown Nests ... 55
Egg With Sunchoke Velouté, Crispy Prosciutto And Hazelnut ... 55
Sausage Scramble ... 58
Eggs Benedict ... 59
Smoked Fish And Poached Egg ... 59
Brioche And Eggs ... 61
Egg Bites ... 62
Sous Vide Scrambled Eggs ... 63
Cured Salmon ... 64

Chapter Nine: Sous Vide Salad Recipes ... 65

Egg And Bacon Salad ... 65
Shrimp Salad ... 67
Waldorf Chicken Salad ... 68
Chicken Caesar Salad ... 69
Salad Lyonnaise ... 70
Garden Vegetable Salad ... 71
Fennel And Orange Quinoa Salad ... 73

    Butternut Squash Salad 75
    Potato Salad With Creamy Rosemary Garlic Butter Dressing 76

Chapter Ten: Sous Vide Soup Recipes 77

    Split Lentil Soup With Smoked Ham Hock 77
    Creamy Celery Soup 79
    Chicken Ramen 80
    Chicken And Vegetable Soup 81
    Wild Mushroom Bisque 82
    Tomato Soup 83
    Beet Soup With Caraway And Yogurt 84
    Sweet Corn And Green Chili Soup 85
    Tri Tip Chili 86
    Borscht 88
    Beef Bourguignon 89
    Beef Burgundy Stew 91

Chapter Eleven: Snack Recipes 93

    Citrus Yogurt 93
    Sous Vide Mushrooms 94
    Sous Vide Corn 95
    Meatballs 96
    Szechuan Pork Belly Bites With BBQ Glaze 97
    Chicken Satay 98
    Tomato Sushi 99
    Lemon-Butter Shrimp 101
    Fresh Vegetables Confit 102
    Escargot Sous Vide 103

Chapter Twelve: Sous Vide Main Course Recipes 105

    Sesame Chicken 105
    Sous Vide Buffalo Chicken Lettuce Wraps 107
    Succulent Sous Vide Chicken With Chili, Ginger And Spring Onion 108
    Spicy Chicken With Smoked Paprika Spice Rub 108
    Chicken Parmigiana 110
    Turkey Breast With Gravy 112
    Mediterranean Turkey Burgers 114
    Sous Vide Turkey Roulade 116
    Sous Vide Steak 117
    Greek Burger With Feta Cream 118
    Short Rib Tacos 120
    Pot Roast 121
    Pork Belly Adobo 122
    Perfect Double-Cut Rosemary Infused Pork Chop With Hard Cider Caramel Sauce 123
    Lamb Chops With Orange 124
    Leg Of Lamb With Rosemary And Garlic 125
    Lamb Chops With Chimichurri Compound Butter 126
    Tilapia With Tomato, Olives And Oregano 127
    Creamy Thai Red Curry With Fish 128
    Sous Vide Lemon Cod 129
    Eggplant Lasagna 130
    Chili-Garlic Tofu 131
    Rotini In Saffron-Tomato Oil 132

Hearty Rice Bowl 133

Chapter Thirteen: Sous Vide Side Dish Recipes 134

Butter-Poached Potatoes 134
Garlic Cheese Risotto 135
Sous Vide Glazed Carrots Recipe 136
Sous Vide Mashed Potatoes 137
Sous Vide Brussels Sprouts 138
Roasted Okra With Curried Lemon Yogurt 139
Swedish Potato Casserole 140
Arroz Braziliero (Brazilian Rice) 141

Chapter Fourteen: Sous Vide Dessert Recipes 142

Chocolate Bean Pots De Crème 142
Pumpkin Pie 143
Red Wine-Poached Pears 144
Strawberry Mousse 145
Grasshopper Cheesecake 146
Rice And Raisin Pudding 147
Salted Caramel Ice Cream 148
Crème Brulee, With Different Flavor Options 149
Brioche Bread Pudding 150

Conclusion 151

References 152

Using Sous Vide To Cook Wagyu 153

Chapter One: About The Wagyu Breed 154

History Of The Breed 154
History Of The Breed In The Us 154
Wagyu In The Us Today 154
Healthy And Delicious Wagyu Beef 155
Using Sous Vide To Cook Wagyu 155

Chapter Two: Wagyu Recipes 157

Wagyu Sous Vide 157
Wagyu Steak 158
Wagyu Brisket With Barbecue Sauce 160

INTRODUCTION

I want to thank you for choosing this book, *Sous Vide - The Complete Cookbook! Best Sous Vide Recipes for Everyone Made Simple.*

The term sous vide might sound extremely complicated and even intimidating. In reality, this is a simple cooking technique that helps enhance and maintain the flavors and textures of different ingredients, unlike any other technique. Vacuum-sealing food in plastic bags and then submerging it in a water bath at a specific temperature can produce brilliant results. Well, this does sound simple, doesn't it? That is precisely what sous vide is all about.

This book will teach you about the basics of sous vide, beginning with what it means, the way it works, and the equipment you require to get started. Additionally, this book is a treasure trove of sorts with plenty of simple and delicious sous vide recipes. Once you understand how this technique works, you can create simple meals that taste exquisite within no time. The recipes in this book are easy to follow and simple to cook. As long as you have stocked your pantry with the ingredients you require, cooking will become easy.

If you are interested in learning about cooking food without losing any of its nutritional value and achieving consistent results every single time, then let us get started!

Thank you once again for choosing this book.

CHAPTER ONE
AN INTRODUCTION TO SOUS VIDE

What is Sous Vide?

In French, the term sous vide means "under a vacuum." Any container from which the air has been completely displaced is known as a vacuum. While using this technique, you will place the ingredients in a plastic bag or a silicone pouch and remove all the air from it, a process known as vacuum sealing. Once the food is vacuum-sealed, it is steeped in a water bath set to a specific temperature. Canning jars made of glass can also be used for sous vide. When the water heats up, the heat is directly transferred to the food inside the sealed bag.

How Does it Work?

Now, it is time for a little science lesson to understand how sous vide actually works. Air is a poor conductor of heat. All the tiny molecules present in the air are set far apart, and are moving constantly. On the other hand, the thermal mass of water is considerably higher. In simpler terms, this means water can absorb and store heat more efficiently than air.

When food is cooked at a constant temperature, it results in uniformity and consistency. For instance, to cook a steak medium rare, the temperature of the water is set within the range required to cook the meat as you desire. It must be somewhere between 131 to 155°F. Once the water bath has reached this temperature, you can place the sealed bag in the water, and the constant heat will gently cook the food from within. The cooking process essentially comes to an end when the core temperature of the ingredient hits the desired heat level.

The integrity of food is often compromised because of three factors — exposure to heat, air, and water. When food is exposed to excessive heat, it results in a chemical reaction that ends up burning or drying out the food. When food is directly placed in water, it not only loses its texture, but its flavor and nutrients, too. Oxidation can change the color, texture, flavor, and nutrient content of various ingredients. By using a vacuum-sealed silicone bag, or a zip-lock pouch, you reduce the chances of compromising the integrity of the ingredients you use. Since the water bath is set at a controlled temperature, it also prevents the food from further damage. The water bath helps in the transference of heat.

Where Does Sous Vide Come From?

Even though sous vide has really gained popularity only in the last couple of years, it's not a new form of cooking—its fundamental principles are actually quite old. Different cultures around the world have various traditional recipes where ingredients are first tightly wrapped and then cooked at low temperatures for extended periods. But the modern era of sous vide, as we know it today, began in the early 1970s. It started when different chefs and researchers in France were looking for a technique that helped to reduce the loss of product while cooking foie gras. Foie gras is an extremely delicate meat that is quite expensive and a popular delicacy in France. However, it tends to lose its textural integrity and flavor profile when exposed to direct heat or water. All this led to the discovery of today's sous vide methodology.

During the mid-1970s, George Pralus, a chef at a restaurant in Roanne, France, developed this technique. When cooked, foie gras tends to lose about 50% of its original mass. Pralus discovered that using sous vide not only improves the texture and appearance of this ingredient, but it also prevented the loss of fat. Sous vide has since become a standard cooking procedure in the best culinary kitchens across the globe. Food lovers are often mesmerized with the beautiful textures and flavors sous vide cooking helps produce. These days, even home cooks can use this technique thanks to readily available information and easy access to the required kitchen equipment.

Why Use Sous Vide?

In this section, let's take a look at the various benefits sous vide offers.

Consistency

While using sous vide, you will cook the dish at a constant temperature, without changing the heat of the water bath. When you cook the food at the same temperature and precisely control it, you will always achieve consistency in your end result. You can effectively attain the same results over and over again by using this technique.

Delicious food

When you cook food using sous vide, your prepared dishes not only look more appealing, but they're tastier, too. By vacuum-sealing food, you reduce the chances of the ingredients losing their form or becoming dehydrated during the cooking process. Using this technique allows you to ensure that the original weight, flavor, color, and textures of the ingredients, along with their aromas, are fully retained. This means you can produce lip-smacking dishes using cheaper cuts of meat and won't necessarily have to splurge on expensive ingredients.

Improves quality

Once you try sous vide, you will realize that food cooked like this is of superior quality when compared to other cooking techniques. You will finally be able to experience food the way it is supposed to be eaten. Since the textual integrity of your ingredients is not compromised during cooking, you can forget about chewy, dry, hard, and soggy meats and vegetables. Sous vide ensures that the meats you cook stay moist and tender, while the vegetables retain their original crunch, texture, and colors.

Better nutrition

As mentioned in the previous point, cooking sous vide certainly makes food taste better. Another advantage of this technique is that it doesn't require extra salt or fat during the cooking process. Once the bag is vacuum-sealed, it prevents the nutrients present in the ingredients from sneaking out during the cooking process. Whenever you steam, deep fry, or boil food, the ingredients lose some of their natural nutrition due to exposure to different elements. In sous vide, the food is never directly in contact with heat—instead, the heat is gently transferred to the food via water. Thanks to the presence of this mediating agent in the cooking process, it prevents the loss of nutrition.

Avoid under or overcooking

When you cook food in a pan, it's quite likely that you might end up overcooking or undercooking one or more of the ingredients used. When exposed to direct heat, food might look perfectly cooked on the outside while it's still raw on the inside. If you try to cook the food until it is well-done on the inside, it might end up being overcooked on the outside. Apart from that, you also stand the risk of burning or scorching the ingredients. By using sous vide, you can prevent the food from being under or overcooked. Sous vide often prescribes a low-temperature cooking, and enables the even distribution of heat.

Easy meals

We all lead extremely hectic lives, and not many of us have the time to cook healthy home-cooked meals on a daily basis. So, preparing easy and nutritious dishes might sound like a blessing. Well, by using sous vide, you will find that cooking your meals becomes quite simple. It is as easy as using a slow cooker. Once you prepare the ingredients, place them in a plastic bag, vacuum-seal it, and, once the water has reached the right temperature, submerge the bag in the water bath. All that's left for you to do is wait for the machine to work its magic and voila, your meal will be ready in no time. You no longer have to spend hours sweating it out in the kitchen to cook a delicious and healthy meal.

Tip: Get started using the different recipes provided in this book, and it will certainly make home cooking much easier than you ever thought possible.

Large quantities

Using sous vide allows you to cook multiple individual portions without any hassle. This certainly makes things easy when it comes to batch cooking. You merely need to divide the ingredients into individual portions, seal them, and place them in the water bath. Yes, it is as simple as that. By spending a couple of hours sous viding your food over the weekend, you can effectively prepare all your meals for the upcoming week.

A great thing about sous vide is that it provides you complete control over timing. You can prepare all the ingredients in advance and then cook your meal whenever you want. If you want, you can allow it to cook slowly in the water bath over an extended period. Maybe you can even complete a couple of chores in the meantime. Since the chances of over or under-cooking the food is quite low, you don't have to worry and can just get on with your work while the machine prepares your meal.

CHAPTER TWO
WHAT DO YOU NEED FOR SOUS VIDE?

Different Sous Vide Machines

Sous vide equipment has been around for decades and is quite popular in professional kitchens. This piece of equipment was rather expensive, bulky, and came with plenty of complicated features. However, with increasing awareness about this popular method of cooking, several sous vide machines were introduced to the consumer market. In this section, let us look at some of the basic types of equipment you can consider while building your very own sous vide setup at home!

Immersion Circulator

An immersion circulator is a kitchen tool that heats water and then circulates it around in the pot while maintaining an even yet precise temperature. Immersion circulators are quite affordable, making these the most popular sous vide machine options today. Since they don't have an inbuilt water bath, they don't take up much space. A standalone device doesn't require any additional equipment, since it can be easily clamped on and adjusted to suit to the pots you use. Some of the best sous vide immersion circulators include the Anova Precision Cooker, Nomiku, ChefSteps Joule, and Sansaire.

Sous Vide Water Oven

The sous vide water oven is a countertop water bath. These are generally the same size as a microwave and are fully contained sous vide devices. A basic sous vide water oven costs at least $500. This device heats water but doesn't circulate it the way an immersion cooker does, which might result in certain inconsistencies while cooking and in the resultant textures, too. AquaChef, Gourmia, and SousVide Supreme are some examples of water ovens. The Instant Pot and other multi-use cookers like Gourmia and Oliso offer sous vide capabilities.

If you're hesitant about investing in a sous vide device right now, then you might want to try DIY sous vide hacks. If you have a rice cooker or a slow cooker at home, you can try a sous vide recipe using a reusable silicone bag that's immersed in water. The results won't be as consistent as what you would see with an immersion cooker, but you will get an idea of how sous vide works.

Sous Vide Packaging

The packaging is an important aspect of sous vide cooking. When food is sealed in containers or bags appropriate for sous vide, these will prevent evaporation while increasing the efficiency of the cooking process. Place all the ingredients as per the recipe in a plastic bag and remove all air present within using a vacuum sealer, immersion technique, or even a straw. You don't even need to invest in a vacuum sealer. Some of the packaging options available include vacuum-sealing bags, resealable bags (like Ziploc's freezer-safe bags), reusable silicone bags, and canning jars.

How to Use Sous Vide?

Sous vide is indeed quite a simple technique, but getting it right does take some practice. In this section, we will learn some tips that will come in handy while using a sous vide machine.

Before you place an ingredient in the pouch, ensure that you have seasoned it thoroughly. While seasoning, however, keep in mind that certain herbs and spices can become overpowering or even go rancid when cooked for extended periods, like garlic, onion greens, pepper, rosemary, thyme, and cumin. Even fresh herbs can lose their original flavor during sous vide cooking, and therefore it is always better to season ingredients with dried herbs.

When the water begins circulating in the water bath, it will eventually start to evaporate. Water will evaporate when it is in constant contact with direct heat for extended periods. Vapor will start gathering within the sous vide machine, which will reduce the level of water in the bath and might even damage the sous vide equipment. If the water level falls, then the cooking process will also be affected. To prevent this, cover the water bath with plastic wrap. This also reduces the chances of heat escaping.

Before you place the bag in the water bath, ensure that it has been vacuum-sealed properly. If there are any air pockets present in the bag, then the resultant dish will not be evenly cooked. The simplest way to check this is by ensuring that the bag is directly in contact with all the ingredients placed within.

The bag can be popped up or down or even shifted above the surface in a circulator. If the bag is properly vacuum-sealed, then it will generally stay submerged. It also depends on the weight of the ingredients you use. If you're cooking an ingredient like fish, the circulator might end up pushing the ingredients around the water bath. Adding any food-safe weights to the vacuum bag is the best way to ensure it always remains submerged.

Perhaps the best way to cook red meat is sous vide. This not only helps retain the natural textures and flavors present in the meat, but also enhances its flavor profile. If you want to extract more flavor from the meat, then always slightly sear your cuts in a pan before vacuum sealing. Alternately, you can also sear the meat after it has cooked in the water bath. Since the bag is vacuum-sealed, all the natural juices will stay contained in the meat. The meat will also start cooking in its own juices, and the residual fats or juices can be used to make a jus to serve on the side.

If you like the idea of cooking juicy and moist chicken every single time, then try sous vide. Cooking chicken at high temperatures ends up charring the external surface while leaving it raw in the middle. When cooked directly on heat, the chances of overcooking the chicken also increase. To avoid all this, opt for sous vide. Once you remove the chicken from the sous vide pouch, sear it on a sizzling hot pan for a couple of seconds. The same technique can be used for cooking pork.

Temperature for Different Meats

Ribeye, Porterhouse, and Strip Steaks

COOK	TEMPERATURE	TIME
Very rare to rare	120°F to 128°F	1 to 2 ½ hours
Medium-rare	129°F to 134°F	1 to 4 hours
Medium	135°F to 144°F	1 to 4 hours
Medium-well	145°F to 155°F	1 to 3 hours
Well done	156°F	1 to 3 hours

Hamburgers

COOK	TEMPERATURE	TIME
Very rare to rare	115°F to 123°F	40 minutes to 2 ½ hours
Medium-rare	124°F to 129°F	40 minutes to 2 ½ hours
Medium	130°F to 137°F	40 minutes to 4 hours
Medium-well	138°F to 144°F	40 minutes to 4 hours
Well done	145°F to 155°F	40 minutes to 3 ½ hours

Tenderloin Steaks

COOK	TEMPERATURE	TIME
Very rare to rare	120°F to 128°F	45 minutes to 2 ½ hours
Medium-rare	129°F to 134°F	45 minutes to 4 hours
Medium	135°F to 144°F	45 minutes to 4 hours
Medium-well	145°F to 155°F	45 minutes to 3 ½ hours
Well done	156°F	1 to 3 hours

Chicken Breasts

COOK	TEMPERATURE	TIME
Tender and juicy (cold salads)	150°F	1 to 4 hours
Very soft and juicy (serve hot)	140°F	1 ½ to 4 hours
Juicy, tender, and a little stringy (serve hot)	150°F	1 to 4 hours
Traditional: juicy, firm, slightly stringy (serve hot)	160°F	1 to 3 hours

Chicken Thighs

COOK	TEMPERATURE	TIME
Firm, juicy, and a little tough	150°F	1 to 4 hours
Tender and very juicy	165°F	1 to 4 hours
Falls-off-the-bone tender	165°F	4 to 8 hours

Pork Chops and Roast

COOK	TEMPERATURE	TIME
Rare	136°F	1 to 3 hours
Medium-rare	144°F	1 to 3 hours
Well done	158°F	1 to 3 hours

Tough Cuts of Pork

COOK	TEMPERATURE	TIME
Rare	140°F	8 to 24 hours
Medium-rare	154°F	8 to 24 hours
Well done	185°F	8 to 24 hours

Pork Ribs

COOK	TEMPERATURE	TIME
Succulent, tender, and meaty	145°F	36 hours
Traditional BBQ	165°F	12 hours

Fish

COOK	TEMPERATURE	TIME
Tender	104°F	40 to 70 minutes
Tender and flaky	122°F	40 to 70 minutes
Well done	131°F	40 to 70 minutes

Vegetables

TYPE	TEMPERATURE	TIME
Green vegetables	180°F	10 to 20 minutes
Root vegetables	185°F	10 to 20 minutes
Winter squash	185°F	10 to 20 minutes

Fruits

TYPE	TEMPERATURE	TIME
Warm and ripe	154°F	1 ¾ hour to 2 ½ hours
Cooked soft (ideal for purees)	185°F	30 minutes to 1 ½ hours

CHAPTER THREE
SOUS VIDE PICKLE RECIPES

Pickled Vegetables

Serves: 20 to 25

Ingredients:

- 24 ounces radishes, rinsed, trimmed, quartered, do not peel
- 1 1/3 cups water
- 2 tablespoons sea salt
- 1 teaspoon yellow or brown mustard seeds
- 4 cloves garlic, peeled, halved lengthwise
- 2 to 4 fresh chili peppers, halved (optional)
- 1 1/3 cups white vinegar
- 6 tablespoons sugar
- 1 teaspoon whole peppercorns
- ½ teaspoon coriander seeds
- 2 bay leaves

Directions:

1. Follow the instructions given in the manual and fill the sous vide water oven. Preheat it to 190°F.
2. Place radishes in a large vacuum-seal pouch or Ziploc bag. Arrange in a single layer.
3. Add the remaining ingredients in a saucepan. Heat over high flame and let it boil. Stir frequently until sugar dissolves completely.
4. Turn off the heat and pour into the pouch. Vacuum seal the pouch.
5. Submerge the pouch in the water bath and set the timer for 45 minutes.

6. Just before the timer goes off, make an ice water bath by filling a large bowl with water and ice.
7. When done, remove the pouch from the water bath and immerse in the ice water bath. When cooled, remove the pouch from the water bath. Empty the contents into an airtight jar.
8. Refrigerate until further use, for up to one week.

Pickled Spring Onions

Serves: 12

Ingredients:

- 2 cups red wine vinegar
- 6 tablespoons kosher salt
- 2 bay leaves
- 16 spring onions, trimmed to the bulbs
- 6 tablespoons very fine sugar
- 2 teaspoons whole peppercorns

Directions:

1. Follow the instructions given in the manual and fill the sous vide water oven. Preheat it to 180°F.
2. Place onions and bay leaves in a large vacuum-seal pouch or Ziploc bag. Arrange in a single layer.
3. Add the remaining ingredients into a bowl and stir well until the sugar dissolves completely.
4. Pour into the pouch and vacuum seal.
5. Submerge the pouch in the water bath and set the timer for 30 minutes.
6. Just before the timer goes off, make an ice water bath by filling a large bowl with water and ice.
7. When done, remove the pouch from the water bath and immerse in the ice water bath. When cooled, remove the pouch from the water bath. Empty the contents into an airtight container.
8. Refrigerate until use, for up to one month.

Pickled Asparagus with Lemon

Serves: 20 to 25

Ingredients:

- 2 bunches asparagus, discard the woody ends
- 3 sprigs dill for each jar
- 2 pieces lemon rind for each jar
- 1 large clove garlic, peeled, crushed, for each jar
- 6 tablespoons kosher salt
- 4 cups apple cider vinegar
- ½ cup lemon juice
- 2 tablespoons sugar

Directions:

1. Follow the instructions given in the manual and fill the sous vide water oven. Preheat it to 145°F.
2. Cut the stalks of asparagus if required to fit into jar. Place asparagus in canning jars. Do not crowd the asparagus. Use more jars if required.
3. Place dill, lemon rind, and garlic cloves in each jar.
4. Add rest of the ingredients into a bowl and stir until sugar dissolves completely.
5. Pour into the jars over the asparagus. Fasten the lids but not too tight. You should be able to open the jars easily.
6. Submerge the jars in the water bath and set the timer for 30 minutes.
7. Take out the jars from the water bath and let them cool to room temperature. These can be stored at room temperature, or you can store them in a container in the refrigerator.

Pickled Kumquats

Serves: 8

Ingredients:

- 2 cups champagne vinegar
- 2 teaspoons pickling spice
- 2 pounds kumquats, halved, deseeded
- 1 cup very fine sugar
- 2 teaspoons grated fresh ginger

Directions:

1. Follow the instructions given in the manual and fill the sous vide water oven. Preheat it to 180°F.
2. Place kumquats in a large vacuum-seal pouch or Ziploc bag.
3. Add rest of the ingredients into a bowl and stir until well combined and sugar dissolves completely.
4. Pour into the pouch and vacuum seal.
5. Submerge the pouch in the water bath and set the timer for 30 minutes.
6. Just before the timer goes off, make an ice water bath by filling a large bowl with water and ice.
7. Take out the pouch from the water bath and let it cool to room temperature. Empty the contents into an airtight container.
8. Refrigerate until use, for up to one month.

Spicy Pickled Pineapple

Serves: 20 to 25

Ingredients:

- 6 ounces small, whole, Brazilian chili peppers
- 2 large purple onions, peeled, cut into round slices
- 4 cups fresh pineapple chunks
- 2 teaspoons pickling spice
- 3 teaspoons ground pink salt or sea salt
- 2 teaspoons ground red pepper
- 2/3 cup apple cider vinegar

Directions:

1. Follow the instructions given in the manual and fill the sous vide water oven. Preheat it to 140°F.
2. Place chili peppers, onions, and pineapple in a large vacuum-seal pouch or Ziploc bag.
3. Add rest of the ingredients into a bowl and stir until well combined.
4. Pour into the pouch and vacuum seal.
5. Submerge the pouch in the water bath and set the timer for 30 minutes.
6. Just before the timer goes off, make an ice water bath by filling a large bowl with water and ice.
7. When done, remove the pouch from the water bath and immerse in the ice water bath. When cooled, remove the pouch from the water bath. Empty the contents into an airtight container.
8. Refrigerate until use, for up to one week.

CHAPTER FOUR
SOUS VIDE JAMS AND PRESERVES

Bourbon-Maple Chutney

Serves: 15 or 16

Ingredients:

- 2 Braeburn apples or any other baking apples, peeled, cored, diced
- 4 tablespoons maple syrup
- 2 tablespoons lemon juice
- 1 teaspoon chipotle chili powder
- 6 tablespoons bourbon
- 2 tablespoons minced thyme leaves
- 2 tablespoons melted butter
- Salt to taste
- Pepper to taste

Directions:

1. Follow the instructions given in the manual and fill the sous vide water oven. Preheat it to 185°F.
2. Add apples into a large vacuum-seal pouch or Ziploc bag.
3. Add rest of the ingredients into a bowl and stir until well combined.
4. Pour into the pouch and vacuum seal. Shake the pouch until well combined.
5. Submerge the pouch in the water bath and set the timer for 1 ½ to 2 hours.
6. Empty the contents into an airtight container. Stir until thick and smooth. Close the container.

7. Refrigerate until use, for up to one week.

Blueberry Compote

Serves: 8 to 10

Ingredients:

- 16 ounces blueberries
- Zest of 2 oranges, grated
- Zest of 2 lemons, grated
- 2 tablespoons honey
- ¼ teaspoon ground cinnamon

Directions:

1. Follow the instructions given in the manual and fill the sous vide water oven. Preheat it to 183°F.
2. Place blueberries, honey, cinnamon, and zests in a large Ziploc bag or vacuum-seal pouch.
3. Vacuum seal the pouch and shake until well combined.
4. Submerge the pouch in the water bath and set the timer for 30 to 60 minutes.
5. When the timer goes off, remove the bag from the water bath. Empty the contents from the pouch into an airtight container. Stir until thick and smooth. Close the container.
6. Refrigerate until use, for up to 10 days.

Spicy Rhubarb Compote

Serves: 15 to 18

Ingredients:

- ½ cup honey
- 2 cups sugar
- 4 cups red wine
- 4 teaspoons red pepper flakes
- ¼ teaspoon salt
- 6 strips (2 inches each) orange peel
- 20 stalks rhubarb, trimmed, cut into 1-inch pieces
- ¼ teaspoon ground cloves (optional)
- ¼ teaspoon ground cinnamon (optional)
- ¼ teaspoon ground cardamom (optional)

Directions:

1. Follow the instructions given in the manual and fill the sous vide water oven. Preheat it to 180°F.
2. Add sugar, wine, pepper flakes, and orange flakes into a saucepan. Place the saucepan over high heat and bring to a boil. Stir frequently until sugar dissolves completely.
3. Add rhubarb and salt into a vacuum-seal pouch or Ziploc bag. Turn off the heat and pour into the pouch. Vacuum seal the pouch.
4. Submerge the pouch in the water bath and set the timer for 45 minutes, or until the stalks are tender.
5. When done, remove the pouch from the water bath. Empty the liquids from the pouch into a saucepan. Heat over medium flame and stir frequently until liquid thickens.
6. Place rhubarb in a shallow bowl. Pour the thickened syrup over the rhubarb. Cover and let it cool to room temperature.
7. Refrigerate until use, for up to one week.

Sous Vide Strawberry-Rhubarb Jam

Serves: 20 to 25

Ingredients:

- 2 cups diced strawberries
- 2 cups diced rhubarb
- 2 cups granulated sugar
- 4 tablespoons fresh lemon juice
- 4 tablespoons powdered pectin

Directions:

1. Follow the instructions given in the manual and fill the sous vide water oven. Preheat it to 180°F.
2. Add strawberries, rhubarb, sugar, lemon juice, and pectin into a large Ziploc bag or vacuum-seal pouch. Press the bag a few times so that the ingredients are well combined.
3. Vacuum seal the pouch.
4. Submerge the pouch in the water bath and set the timer for 90 minutes.
5. When done, remove the pouch from the water bath. Empty the contents of the pouch into an airtight container. Cool completely.
6. Refrigerate until use, for up to 10 days.

Sous Vide Peaches

Serves: 12

Ingredients:

- 6 pounds peaches, peeled, pitted, sliced
- 1 cup white wine
- 12 tablespoons sugar
- 8 teaspoons torn rose geranium leaves or 1 teaspoon vanilla extract or a 3-inch stick cinnamon

Directions:

1. Follow the instructions given in the manual and fill the sous vide water oven. Preheat it to 150°F.
2. Place all the ingredients in a large vacuum-seal pouch or Ziploc bag. Press the bag a few times so that the ingredients are well combined.
3. Vacuum seal the pouch.
4. Submerge the pouch in the water bath and set the timer for 45 minutes.
5. When done, remove the pouch from the water bath. Empty the contents of the pouch into an airtight container. Cool completely.
6. Refrigerate until use, for up to 10 days.

Raspberry Preserves

Serves: 12 to 15

Ingredients:

- 4 cups fresh raspberries
- 1 cup granulated sugar
- 2 teaspoons grated fresh lemon zest
- 6 tablespoons tapioca starch
- 2 teaspoons fresh lemon juice
- 2 teaspoons pure vanilla extract

Directions:

1. Follow the instructions given in the manual and fill the sous vide water oven. Preheat it to 190°F.
2. Place all the ingredients in a large vacuum-seal pouch or Ziploc bag. Press the bag a few times so that the ingredients are well combined.
3. Vacuum seal the pouch.
4. Submerge the pouch in the water bath and set the timer for 45 minutes.
5. Just before the timer goes off, make an ice water bath by filling a large bowl with water and ice.
6. When done, remove the pouch from the water bath and immerse in the ice water bath. When cooled, remove the pouch from the water bath. Empty the contents into an airtight container.
7. Refrigerate until use, for up to 10 days.

Strawberry-Basil Maple Syrup

Serves: 20 to 25

Ingredients:

- 4 cups pure maple syrup
- 2 cups loosely-packed basil leaves
- 16 ounces strawberries, sliced
- 1 teaspoon fine sea salt

Directions:

1. Follow the instructions given in the manual and fill the sous vide water oven. Preheat it to 135°F.
2. Add all the ingredients into a vacuum-seal pouch or Ziploc bag.
3. Vacuum seal the pouch.
4. Submerge the pouch in the water bath and set the timer for 60 minutes.
5. When done remove from the water bath and let it cool for a few minutes. When the syrup is cool enough to handle, discard the basil leaves.
6. Empty the rest of the contents into an airtight container.
7. Refrigerate until use, for up to 10 days.

CHAPTER FIVE
SOUS VIDE SAUCES

Cranberry Sauce

Serves: 10 to 15

Ingredients:

- 14.1 ounces fresh cranberries
- Zest of 1 orange, grated
- ⅓ cup granulated sugar

Directions:

1. Follow the instructions given in the manual and fill the sous vide water oven. Preheat it to 185°F.
2. Add all the ingredients into a vacuum-seal pouch or Ziploc bag.
3. Vacuum seal the pouch.
4. Submerge the pouch in the water bath. Place something heavy on the pouch, as the cranberries tend to float. Set the timer for 45 minutes.
5. Just before the timer goes off, make an ice water bath by filling a large bowl with water and ice.
6. When done, remove the pouch from the water bath and immerse in the ice water bath. When cooled, remove the pouch from the water bath. Press the pouch at a few places so that the cranberries are slightly crushed. Empty the contents into an airtight container.
7. Refrigerate until use, for up to 10 days.

Tomato Basil Pasta Sauce

Serves: 12 to 15

Ingredients:

- 2 cans crushed tomatoes
- 1 white onion, finely chopped
- 2 tablespoons extra-virgin olive oil
- 6 bay leaves
- 4 cups fresh basil leaves
- 2 carrots, peeled, finely chopped
- 2 teaspoons garlic salt
- 2 teaspoons red pepper flakes

Directions:

1. Follow the instructions given in the manual and fill the sous vide water oven. Preheat it to 185°F.
2. Add all the ingredients into a vacuum-seal pouch or Ziploc bag.
3. Vacuum seal the pouch.
4. Submerge the pouch in the water bath. Adjust the timer for 90 minutes.
5. When done, remove from the water bath and let it cool for a few minutes.
6. Transfer into a blender and blend until smooth. Serve over hot cooked pasta.
7. Cool completely the leftovers and transfer into an airtight container. Refrigerate until use, for up to 4 days.

Béarnaise Sauce

Serves: 4 to 6

Ingredients:

- ¼ cup chopped tarragon
- 12 whole peppercorns
- 1 1/3 cups dry vermouth or dry white wine
- 4 tablespoons water
- ¼ cup chopped shallot
- 4 tablespoons white wine vinegar
- 8 egg yolks
- 1 ¼ cups butter, melted

Directions:

1. Follow the instructions given in the manual and fill the sous vide water oven. Preheat it to 174°F.
2. Add shallot, tarragon, vinegar, peppercorns, and wine into a saucepan and place over medium-high heat.
3. Boil until the liquid reduces to approximately 6 tablespoons, then turn off the heat. Strain into a bowl and discard the solids.
4. Add yolks into a bowl and beat lightly. Add melted butter, water and strained liquid and whisk well. Transfer into a large vacuum-seal pouch or Ziploc bag.
5. Vacuum seal the pouch.
6. Submerge the pouch in the water bath. Adjust the timer for 45 minutes.
7. When done, remove from the water bath and transfer into a bowl. Whisk well. If you find the sauce too thick, add a little water to dilute.
8. Use as desired. Cool any leftovers completely and transfer into an airtight container. Refrigerate until use, for up to 4 days.

Tomato Sauce

Serves: 5 or 6

Ingredients:

- 4 tablespoons olive oil
- 1 cup chopped onions
- 6 sprigs oregano
- 6 whole sprigs fresh thyme
- 6 whole sprigs fresh thyme
- 2/3 cup chopped parsley
- 12 large basil leaves

Directions:

1. Follow the instructions given in the manual and fill the sous vide water oven. Preheat it to 182°F.
2. Heat a skillet over medium flame and add some oil. Once the oil is warm, add onion, garlic, shallot, and oregano, and sauté until onions become translucent. Turn off the heat, then add the rest of the ingredients and mix well.
3. Transfer into a large Ziploc bag or vacuum-seal pouch.
4. Vacuum seal the pouch.
5. Submerge the pouch in the water bath. Adjust the timer for 50 minutes.
6. When the timer goes off, remove the bag from the water bath. Empty the contents from the pouch into an airtight container.
7. Refrigerate until use, for up to 10 days.

CHAPTER SIX
SOUS VIDE INFUSIONS, CANNING BEANS AND GRAINS

Infused Olive Oil

Makes: 4 cups

Ingredients:

- Herbs or spices of your choice, like basil, chili, etc., for infusion
- 4 cups olive oil or any other vegetable oil of your choice

Directions:

1. Follow the instructions given in the manual and fill the sous vide water oven. Preheat it to 131°F.
2. Pour oil into a vacuum-seal pouch. Add your infusion ingredients.
3. Vacuum seal the pouch.
4. Submerge the pouch in the water bath and set the timer for 3 hours.
5. When done, remove the pouch from the water bath. Let the oil cool and strain if desired. Empty the contents into a bottle, and fasten the lid.
6. Refrigerate until use, for up to 2 months.

Infused Vinegar

Makes: About 3 cups

Ingredients:

- Zest of 2 lemons
- 2 shallots, minced
- 1 cup tarragon leaves
- 25 ounces white wine vinegar

Directions:

1. Follow the instructions given in the manual and fill the sous vide water oven. Preheat it to 135°F.
2. Add all the ingredients into a vacuum-seal pouch or Mason jar.
3. Vacuum seal the pouch or fasten the lid lightly.
4. Submerge the pouch in the water bath and set the timer for 2 hours.
5. When done, remove the pouch or jar from the water bath and let it cool. When cooled, strain into a separate jar, discarding the solids. Fasten the lid.
6. Refrigerate until use, for up to 12 days.

Grains in Canning Jars

Serves: 4

Ingredients:

- 1 cup whole grains like quinoa, steel-cut oats, or brown rice
- 1 teaspoon kosher salt
- 1 ½ cups warm water for quinoa or rice and 2 cups water for oats

Directions:

1. Follow the instructions given in the manual and fill the sous vide water oven. Preheat it to 180°F.
2. Take a large canning jar. Add your grains and water accordingly. Add salt and stir.
3. Fasten the lid lightly, but not tight at all.
4. Submerge the canning jar in water bath and adjust the timer for 3 hours.
5. When done, remove the jars from the water bath and cool completely.
6. Use as required or place in the refrigerator until use.

Sous Vide Navy Beans, With Prior Soaking

Serves: 2 or 3

Ingredients:

- 3.5 ounces dry navy beans
- ½ teaspoon salt + extra for cooking
- 18 ounces water + extra for cooking

Directions:

1. Follow the instructions given in the manual and fill the sous vide water oven. Preheat it to 194°F.
2. Add beans into a container and top with 18 ounces water. Cover and place in the refrigerator for 16 to 24 hours.
3. Remove from the refrigerator and drain. Rinse a couple of times.
4. Place beans in a vacuum-seal pouch or Ziploc bag. Add a cup of water and ½ teaspoon salt.
5. Submerge the pouch in the water bath and adjust the timer for 90 minutes. After about 80 minutes of cooking, remove the bag and press the beans (through the bag) and check if they are cooked. If the beans are cooked, switch off the water bath; if not, continue cooking until the beans are tender.
6. When the timer goes off, remove the bag from the water bath. Empty the contents from the pouch into an airtight container.
7. Refrigerate until use, for up to 4 days.

Sous Vide Beans, Without Soaking

Serves: 8

Ingredients:

- 2 cups dried pinto beans, rinsed
- 4 cloves garlic, crushed
- 2 teaspoons kosher salt
- 1 onion, halved
- 2 teaspoons dried oregano
- 6 cups water

To serve:

- Cayenne pepper
- Sour cream

Directions:

1. Follow the instructions given in the manual and fill the sous vide water oven. Preheat it to 190°F.
2. Add all the ingredients into a vacuum-seal pouch or Ziploc bag.
3. Vacuum seal the pouch.
4. Submerge the pouch in the water bath and adjust the timer for 6 hours. After about 5 hours of cooking, remove the bag and press the beans (through the bag) and check if they are cooked. If the beans are cooked, switch off the water bath; if not, continue cooking until the beans are tender.
5. When done, remove from the water bath and let cool for a few minutes. Drain off the liquid and remove the onion and garlic.
6. Refrigerate until use, for up to 4 days.
7. To serve: Warm the beans and drizzle with sour cream. Sprinkle cayenne pepper on top and serve.

Lentils in Canning Jars

Serves: 8

Ingredients:

- 2 cups dried lentils, rinsed
- 2 teaspoons kosher salt
- Warm water as required
- 2 bay leaves

Directions:

1. Follow the instructions given in the manual and fill the sous vide water oven. Preheat it to 190°F.
2. Take a large canning jar. Add lentils. Pour warm water into the jar (fill up to the neck).
3. Add bay leaves and salt into the jar. You can use 2 jars if you do not have a large enough jar.
4. Fasten the lid lightly, but not very tight.
5. Submerge the canning jars in water bath and adjust the timer for 2 hours.
6. When done, remove the jar and cool completely.
7. Discard the bay leaves.
8. Use as required or cool completely and refrigerate until use, for up to 4 days.

CHAPTER SEVEN
SOUS VIDE BEVERAGE RECIPES

Spiked Hot Chocolate

Serves: 4

Ingredients:

For peppermint whipped cream:

- A drop peppermint extract
- 2 cups heavy cream, chilled
- 4 tablespoons crushed peppermint candy, to garnish

For spiked hot chocolate:

- 1 ½ cups whole milk
- ¼ cup butterscotch schnapps
- 2 tablespoons sugar (optional)
- 4 ounces good quality 70% dark chocolate
- 1 cup heavy cream
- 2 tablespoons dark rum or bourbon
- ½ tablespoon vanilla extract

Directions:

1. For whipped cream: Add cream and peppermint extract into a bowl. Beat well until stiff peaks are formed. Chill until use.
2. Follow the instructions given in the manual and fill the sous vide water oven. Preheat it

to 185°F.
3. Add all the ingredients for spiked hot chocolate into a vacuum-seal pouch or Ziploc bag.
4. Vacuum seal the pouch.
5. Submerge the pouch in the water bath. Adjust the timer for 50 minutes or until chocolate melts completely.
6. When the timer goes off, remove the bag from the water bath. Empty the contents from the pouch into a bowl and whisk well.
7. Pour into glasses and spoon some whipped cream on top. Scatter the crushed peppermint on top and serve.

Ponche Crema

Serves: 5 or 6

Ingredients:

- 2 eggs, beaten well
- ½ can (from a 14-ounce can) sweetened condensed milk
- 1 cup water
- 6 ounces canned evaporated milk
- 1 cup white rum
- 6 ounces canned crème de coco (coconut cream)
- 2 sticks cinnamon
- Ground cinnamon to garnish

Directions:

1. Follow the instructions given in the manual and fill the sous vide water oven. Preheat it to 185°F.
2. Add all the ingredients except cinnamon sticks into a blender and blend until smooth.
3. Pour into a Ziploc or vacuum-seal cooking pouch. Add cinnamon sticks.
4. Vacuum seal the pouch.
5. Submerge the pouch in the water bath. Set the timer for 2 hours.
6. Just before the timer goes off, make an ice water bath by filling a large bowl with water and ice.
7. When done, remove the pouch from the water bath and immerse in the ice water bath. When cooled, remove the pouch from the water bath.
8. Strain the liquid and discard the solids. Pour into a jug.
9. Chill until use.
10. To serve: Pour into a large bowl. Add rum and stir well. Sprinkle cinnamon on top.
11. Pour into individual glasses and enjoy.

Sous Vide 'Cold' Brew Coffee

Serves: 3

Ingredients:

- 2 cups water
- ¼ cup freshly ground coarse coffee

Directions:

1. Follow the instructions given in the manual and fill the sous vide water oven. Preheat it to 150°F.

2. Add coffee grounds into a Mason jar and pour water over it. Fasten the lid lightly, not tight.
3. Submerge the jar in the water bath. Set the timer for 2 hours.
4. Pour into a coffee filter. Once filtered, pour into a Mason jar.
5. Refrigerate until use, for up to 10 days.

Limoncello

Serves: 6

Ingredients:

- 5 fresh lemons, rinse well
- 2 cups water
- 2 cups vodka
- ¾ cup very fine sugar

Directions:

1. Follow the instructions given in the manual and fill the sous vide water oven. Preheat it to 135°F.
2. Remove lemon zest with a peeler, but do not peel the pith. Use the lemons in some other recipe.
3. Add lemon strips and vodka into a Ziploc bag or vacuum-seal pouch.
4. Vacuum seal the pouch.
5. Submerge the pouch in the water bath. Adjust the timer for 2 hours.
6. Remove the pouch from the water bath and let it cool completely. Strain the mixture into a bowl and discard the solids.
7. Meanwhile, make the syrup as follows: Add water and sugar into a saucepan and place over medium-high heat. Stir frequently until the sugar dissolves.
8. When it comes to a boil, turn off the heat and let it cool completely.
9. Add into the bowl of limoncello. Stir until well combined. Pour into a clean bottle. Fasten the lid. Refrigerate until use.

Eggnog

Serves: 4

Ingredients:

- 3 large eggs
- ½ cup heavy cream
- ¼ cup brandy
- ¼ cup bourbon
- ¼ cup very fine sugar
- ¼ teaspoon freshly ground nutmeg + extra to serve
- 1/8 teaspoon kosher salt
- ½ quart whole milk
- ½ teaspoon vanilla bean paste
- ¼ teaspoon freshly ground cinnamon

Directions:

1. Follow the instructions given in the manual and fill the sous vide water oven. Preheat it to 144°F.
2. Add all the ingredients into a blender and blend until smooth.
3. Pour into a Ziploc bag or vacuum-seal pouch.
4. Vacuum seal the pouch.
5. Submerge the pouch in the water bath. Set the timer for 45 minutes.
6. Remove the pouch from the water bath a few times during this time and turn the bag around to mix well.
7. Just before the timer goes off, make an ice water bath by filling a large bowl with water and ice.
8. When done, remove the pouch from the water bath and immerse in the ice water bath. When cooled, remove the pouch from the water.
9. Pour into glasses and serve right away.
10. Leftovers can be stored in a jar in the refrigerator for up to 3 days.

Jalapeño Vodka

Serves: 5 or 6

Ingredients:

- ½ bottle (from a 25-ounce bottle) vodka
- 1 fresh jalapeño, halved lengthwise, discard seeds and membranes

To make Spicy Bloody Mary – per serving:

- 2 ounces jalapeño vodka

- 1 ounce lemon juice
- A dash Worcestershire sauce
- 4 ounces vegetable or tomato juice cocktail
- ½ tablespoon horseradish (optional)
- Celery salt and black pepper to rim the glasses
- Olives to garnish
- Green beans to garnish (optional)
- Ice cubes, as required

Directions:

1. Follow the instructions given in the manual and fill the sous vide water oven. Preheat it to 147°F.
2. Add peppers and vodka into a large vacuum-seal pouch or Ziploc bag. Vacuum seal the pouch.
3. Submerge the pouch into the water bath and set the timer for 1 ½ hours. Remove the pouch a few times while it is cooking to shake it before placing it back in the water bath.
4. Just before the timer goes off, make an ice water bath by filling a large bowl with water and ice.
5. When done, remove the pouch from the water bath and immerse in the ice water bath. When cooled, remove the pouch from the water.
6. Pass the mixture through a sieve and discard the solids.
7. Pour into a bottle. Fasten the lid and refrigerate until use, for up to one month.
8. To serve: Mix together celery salt and pepper on a plate. Dip the rim of the glasses in water and dredge the rim on the celery salt mixture. Set aside.
9. In a pitcher, mix together vodka, tomato juice cocktail, Worcestershire sauce, lemon juice, and horseradish. Add ice and mix well.
10. Place a few cubes of ice in each glass. Pour cocktail into the glasses.
11. Garnish with olives and green beans and serve.

Pear Shrub

Makes: About 32 ounces

Ingredients:

- 16 ounces Bosc pears, cored, thinly sliced or chopped with the peel on
- 16 ounces apple cider vinegar
- 16 ounces sugar

Directions:

1. Follow the instructions given in the manual and fill the sous vide water oven. Preheat it to 148°F.
2. Add sugar and pears into a large vacuum-seal pouch or Ziploc bag. Use 2 smaller pouches if it will not fit in a large pouch.
3. Vacuum seal the pouch.
4. Submerge the pouch into the water bath and set the timer for 1 hour.
5. Just before the timer goes off, make an ice water bath by filling a large bowl with water and ice.
6. When done, remove the pouch from the water bath and immerse in the ice water bath. When cooled, remove the pouch from the water bath.
7. Pour apple cider vinegar and vacuum seal the pouch once again.
8. Immerse the pouch in the water bath and set timer for 6 hours.
9. Just before the timer goes off, make an ice water bath by filling a large bowl with water and ice.
10. When done, remove the pouch from the water bath and immerse in the ice water bath. When cooled, remove the pouch from the water bath.
11. Place pouch in the refrigerator for 2 to 3 hours.
12. Strain the mixture through a wire mesh strainer placed over a jug. Pour into bottles with stopper.
13. Refrigerate until use. You can use the pears in some other recipe.

Raspberry Cordial

Serves: 8

Ingredients:

- 1 cup fresh raspberries
- 1 ½ cups vodka
- 1 cup sugar

Directions:

1. Follow the instructions given in the manual and fill the sous vide water oven. Preheat it to 135°F.
2. Mix together sugar and raspberries in a vacuum-seal pouch or Ziploc bag. Mash it slightly with your hands. Add vodka into the pouch. Vacuum seal the pouch.
3. Submerge the pouch in the water bath and set timer for 2 hours.
4. When the timer goes off, remove from the water bath and cool completely. Pass the mixture through a fine wire mesh strainer placed over a jug and discard the solids.
5. Pour into a bottle with a stopper. Fasten a lid and refrigerate until use.

Sorrel Punch (Jamaican Christmas Punch)

Makes: About 24 ounces

Ingredients:

- 1 cup dried sorrel (hibiscus flowers)
- ½ tablespoon whole allspice berries
- 2 cups water
- 2 tablespoons fresh, minced ginger
- ½ cup caster sugar

Directions:

1. Follow the instructions given in the manual and fill the sous vide water oven. Preheat it to 135°F.
2. Add all the ingredients into a vacuum-seal pouch or Ziploc bag.
3. Vacuum seal the pouch.
4. Submerge the pouch in the water bath. Set the timer for 30 minutes.
5. Just before the timer goes off, make an ice water bath by filling a large bowl with water and ice.
6. When done, remove the pouch from the water bath and immerse in the ice water bath. When cooled, remove the pouch from the water bath.
7. Strain the mixture through a wire mesh strainer placed over a jug. Pour into a bottle with a stopper and discard the solids.
8. Refrigerate until use.

CHAPTER EIGHT
BREAKFAST RECIPES

Overnight Oatmeal

Serves: 4

Ingredients:

- 2/3 cup rolled oats
- 2/3 cup pinhead oatmeal
- 1 1/3 cups milk or cream
- 4 teaspoons raisins
- 2 cups water
- 2 teaspoons maple syrup or honey

Directions:

1. Follow the instructions given in the manual and fill the sous vide water oven. Preheat it to 140°F.
2. Take 4 Mason jars or glass jam jars with lids. Divide the oats and pinhead oatmeal (you can also use quick-cook steel-cut oats) among the jars. Divide the milk and pour over the oats. Pour ½ cup water in each jar.
3. Add a teaspoon of raisins to each jar. Fasten the lids lightly, not tight.
4. Immerse the filled jars in the water bath. The lids of the jars should be above the level of water in the cooker. This is important.
5. Set the timer for 9 to 10 hours.
6. When done, stir and serve with some butter, if desired.

Overnight Oatmeal with Stewed Fruit Compote

Serves: 4

Ingredients:

For oatmeal:

- 2 cups quick-cooking rolled oats
- ¼ teaspoon ground cinnamon
- 6 cups water
- A pinch salt

For Stewed Fruit Compote:

- 1½ cups mixed dried fruit of your choice—cherries, apricots, cranberries, etc.
- 1 cup water
- Zest of an orange, finely grated
- Zest of a lemon, finely grated
- ¼ cup white sugar
- ¼ teaspoon vanilla extract

Directions:

1. Follow the instructions given in the manual and fill the sous vide water oven. Preheat it to 155°F.
2. Place oatmeal, water, salt, and cinnamon in a vacuum-seal pouch or Ziploc bag.
3. Place all the ingredients of the fruit compote in another similar pouch, and vacuum seal both.
4. Submerge both pouches in the water bath and set the timer for 6 to 10 hours.
5. Remove the pouches and shake them well.
6. Divide the oatmeal into 4 bowls. Top with fruit compote and serve.

French Toast

Serves: 8

Ingredients:

- 8 slices bread
- 1 cup heavy cream
- 1 teaspoon ground cinnamon
- 4 eggs
- 2 teaspoons vanilla extract

For finishing:

- ½ cup butter

Directions:

1. Follow the instructions given in the manual and fill the sous vide water oven. Preheat it to 147°F.
2. Add eggs, vanilla, cream, and cinnamon into a bowl and whisk well.
3. Dip the bread slices in the egg mixture, one at a time, and place in a large vacuum-seal pouch or Ziploc bag. Use 2 bags, if desired. Place in a single layer.
4. Vacuum seal the pouch.
5. Submerge the pouch in the water bath. Set the timer for 60 minutes.
6. Remove the pouch from the water bath and remove the bread slices from the pouch.
7. For finishing: Place a large skillet over medium heat.
8. Add 1 or 2 tablespoons butter. When butter melts, place 2 or 3 bread slices on the pan and cook to desired doneness.

Perfect Egg Tostada

Serves: 4

Ingredients:

- 4 large eggs, at room temperature
- ¼ cup cooked or canned black beans, heated
- 4 sprigs cilantro, chopped
- 4 corn tostadas
- 4 teaspoons salsa taquera or salsa Verde or chili de arbol
- 4 teaspoons queso fresco, crumbled

Directions:

1. Follow the instructions given in the manual and fill the sous vide water oven. Preheat it to 162°F.
2. Place the eggs on a spoon, one at a time, and gently lower them into the water bath and place on the rack. Set the timer for 15 minutes.
3. When the timer goes off, immediately remove the eggs from the water bath. Place the eggs in a bowl of cold water for a few minutes.
4. To assemble: Place the tostadas on 4 serving plates. Spread a tablespoon of beans over it, then salsa, then sprinkle cheese on top and serve.

Poached Eggs in Hash Brown Nests

Serves: 3

Ingredients:

- 6 large eggs, at room temperature
- 3 cups frozen shredded hash brown, thawed completely
- 1 teaspoon fresh rosemary, chopped, or ¼ teaspoon dried rosemary
- Freshly ground pepper to taste
- Salt to taste
- 2 tablespoons chopped fresh chives
- 1 ½ tablespoons extra-virgin olive oil
- ¼ teaspoon paprika
- 3 thin slices prosciutto, halved crosswise
- Cooking spray

Directions:

1. Follow the instructions given in the manual and fill the sous vide water oven. Preheat it to 147°F.
2. Place the eggs on a spoon, one at a time, and gently lower them into the water bath and place on the lower rack. Set the timer for 60 minutes.
3. Meanwhile, grease a 6-count muffin pan with cooking spray.
4. Place hash browns on a kitchen towel. Squeeze out as much moisture as possible.
5. Place the hash browns in a bowl. Add oil, rosemary, pepper, paprika, and salt. Mix well.
6. Divide this mixture among the muffin cups. Press down at the bottom and sides of the muffin cups. Spray cooking spray over it.
7. Preheat oven to 375°F.
8. Place the muffin tin in the oven and bake for about 30 minutes or until nearly golden brown.
9. Place half slice of prosciutto over each hash brown. Let it hang from the edges of the hash brown nests. Bake for 5 minutes.
10. Remove from the oven and cool for 4 or 5 minutes. Run a knife around the edges of the hash brown nest and gently lift it out from the muffin tin.
11. When the timer of the sous vide cooker goes off, immediately remove the eggs. Break 2 cooked eggs in each nest. Garnish with chives and serve immediately.

Egg with Sunchoke Velouté, Crispy Prosciutto and Hazelnut

Serves: 3

Ingredients:

For sunchoke velouté:

- 2 tablespoons butter
- 1 small leek, only white part, thinly sliced
- 1 pound Jerusalem artichokes (sunchokes), peeled, sliced
- ½ quart milk
- ¼ cup heavy cream (optional)
- 1 medium onion, thinly sliced
- 1 clove garlic, sliced
- ½ quart chicken stock
- ¼ vanilla bean, scraped

For bouquet garni:

- 2 or 3 thyme sprigs
- 2 or 3 fresh sage leaves
- 1 bay leaf
- Leek greens, to wrap

For sous vide eggs:

- 3 eggs, at room temperature

For finishing:

- 3 thin slices prosciutto
- Few strips fried Jerusalem artichokes (sunchokes)
- A handful baby watercress
- 6 hazelnuts, toasted, chopped
- Oil, as required

Directions:

1. Follow the instructions given in the manual and fill the sous vide water oven. Preheat it to 145°F.
2. Place the eggs on a spoon and gently lower them into the water bath. Place on the lower rack. Set the timer for 47 minutes.
3. Meanwhile, make the sunchoke velouté as follows: Place a casserole dish over medium flame. Add butter. When butter melts, add onion, garlic, leeks, salt and pepper.
4. To make bouquet garni, place together thyme, sage, and bay leaf and wrap it with leek greens.
5. Place bouquet garni in the casserole dish. Cook for a few minutes.
6. Stir in the artichokes and cook until slightly tender. Stir occasionally.
7. Add rest of the ingredients and stir. Once it boils, reduce the flame and let it simmer until tender. Turn off the heat and remove the bouquet garni.
8. Blend the mixture in a blender. Strain the mixture through a wire mesh strainer placed over a saucepan.
9. To finish: Smear oil over the prosciutto slices and lay them on a lined baking sheet.

10. Bake in a preheated oven at 300°F until crisp. Remove from the oven and cool.
11. Place a few strips of sunchoke on a nonstick pan. Add a bit of oil. Add sunchoke and cook until crisp. Sprinkle salt.
12. Crack a cooked egg into each of 3 bowls.
13. Spoon the sunchoke velouté over the eggs in each bowl.
14. Serve topped with prosciutto, hazelnuts, watercress, and fried sunchoke strips.

Sausage Scramble

Serves: 3

Ingredients:

- 16 large eggs, well beaten
- 8 ounces breakfast sausages, crumbled
- 4 tablespoons butter
- Salt and pepper, as per taste
- ½ cup Mexican cheese, grated

Directions:

1. Follow the instructions given in the manual and fill the sous vide water oven. Preheat it to 165°F.
2. Place a skillet over medium heat and cook the sausages until they are browned.
3. Transfer the cooked sausages in a bowl lined with paper towels and allow them to cool. Once the sausages cool, place them in a Ziploc bag. Add the eggs, butter, cheese, salt and pepper and vacuum seal the bag.
4. Submerge and cook in the sous vide cooker for around 20 minutes. Take the pouch out occasionally and shake the contents well before submerging again. Cook until the eggs are as per your liking.
5. Remove from the water bath and serve.

Eggs Benedict

Serves: 4

Ingredients:

- 4 English muffins, halved, toasted
- 8 slices Canadian bacon
- A handful fresh parsley, chopped
- 8 eggs
- Butter, as required

For hollandaise sauce:

- 8 tablespoons butter
- 2 teaspoons lemon juice
- 1 shallot, diced
- Salt to taste
- Cayenne pepper to taste
- 2 egg yolks
- 2 teaspoons water

Directions:

1. Follow the instructions given in the manual and fill the sous vide water oven. Preheat it to 148°F.
2. Place the eggs in a vacuum-seal pouch or Ziploc bag. Place all the ingredients for hollandaise sauce into another bag. Vacuum seal the pouches.
3. Submerge both pouches in the water bath and set the timer for 1 hour.
4. Meanwhile, cook the bacon in a pan to the desired doneness. Keep warm in an oven along with muffins if desired.
5. Remove the pouches from the water bath. Transfer the contents of the sauce into a blender and blend until smooth.
6. Place muffins on individual serving plates. Crack an egg on each muffin and place on the bottom half of the muffins.
7. Spoon hollandaise over the eggs and garnish with parsley. Cover with the top half of the muffins and serve.

Smoked Fish and Poached Egg

Serves: 4

Ingredients:

- 4 fillets smoked fish

- 2 lemons, cut into slices
- Seasonings of your choice
- 4 large eggs
- 4 tablespoons olive oil

Directions:

1. Follow the instructions given in the manual and fill the sous vide water oven. Preheat it to 140°F.
2. Divide all the ingredients except eggs into 4 vacuum-seal pouches or Ziploc bags.
3. Seal the pouches, but do not remove the air completely.
4. Submerge both pouches in the water bath and set the timer for 20 minutes.
5. When the timer goes off, remove the pouches and set aside.
6. Increase the temperature to 167°F.
7. Place the eggs on a spoon, one at a time, and gently lower them into the water bath and place on the lower rack. Set the timer for 15 minutes.
8. Empty each pouch onto individual serving plates. Break an egg over each fillet and serve.

Brioche and Eggs

Serves: 6

Ingredients:

- 6 brioche buns
- 6 large eggs
- 2 scallions, sliced (optional)
- 1 ½ cups grated cheese

Directions:

1. Follow the instructions given in the manual and fill the sous vide water oven. Preheat it to 149°F.
2. Place the eggs on a spoon, one at a time, and gently lower them into the water bath and place on the rack. Set the timer for 45 minutes.
3. When the timer goes off, immediately remove the eggs from the water bath. Place the eggs in a bowl of cold water for a few minutes.
4. Place brioche buns on a baking sheet and break a cooked egg on each bun. Sprinkle cheese on top.
5. Set an oven to broil and place the baking sheet in the oven. Broil for few minutes until cheese melts.

Egg Bites

Serves: 4

Ingredients:

- 5 eggs
- ¼ cup shredded Colby Jack cheese
- 3 tablespoons unsweetened almond milk
- Salt to taste
- Pepper to taste

Directions:

1. Follow the instructions given in the manual and fill the sous vide water oven. Preheat it to 172°F.
2. Add a tablespoon of cheese into each of 4 canning jars or Mason jars.
3. Whisk together eggs and milk in a bowl. Divide the egg mixture among the jars. Season with salt and pepper.
4. Fasten the lid lightly, not very tight.
5. Submerge the canning jars in water bath and adjust the timer for 1 hour or until eggs are set.
6. Remove the jars from the water bath. Serve directly from the jars.

Sous Vide Scrambled Eggs

Serves: 4

Ingredients:

- 8 large eggs
- Freshly ground pepper to taste
- Salt to taste
- Aleppo pepper to taste (optional)
- 2 tablespoons butter

Directions:

1. Follow the instructions given in the manual and fill the sous vide water oven. Preheat it to 165°F.
2. Add eggs, salt, and pepper into a bowl and whisk well. Pour into a large silicone bag and vacuum seal the pouch.
3. Submerge the pouch in the water bath and adjust the timer for 10 minutes.
4. Remove the pouch from the water bath and place the pouch between your palms. Press it and shake it.
5. Place it back in the water bath. Set the timer for 12 minutes.
6. When the timer goes off, remove the pouch from the water bath.
7. Open the pouch and divide onto 4 plates.
8. Garnish with Aleppo pepper. Serve immediately.

Cured Salmon

Serves: 2

Ingredients:

- 2 salmon fillets (6 ounces each)
- 8 tablespoons sugar
- 8 tablespoons salt
- 2 teaspoons smoke flavor powder (optional)

Directions:

1. Take 2 bowls and place a fillet in each bowl.
2. Divide the sugar, salt and smoke flavor powder among the bowls. Mix well. Set aside for 30 minutes.
3. Rinse the fillets in water.
4. Place in a large Ziploc bag. Vacuum seal the pouch.
5. Submerge the pouch in the water bath and adjust the timer for 30 minutes.
6. Just before the timer goes off, make an ice water bath by filling a large bowl with water and ice.
7. When done, remove the pouch from the water bath and immerse in the ice water bath. When cooled, remove the pouch from the water bath.
8. Remove the fillets from the pouch and serve.

CHAPTER NINE
SOUS VIDE SALAD RECIPES

Egg and Bacon Salad

Serves: 8

Ingredients:

For salad:

- 8 ounces bacon, cut into cubes
- 8 eggs
- 8 cups baby mesclun
- 2 small radicchio, cored, thinly sliced

For dressing:

- 4 tablespoons champagne vinegar
- 1 tablespoon honey
- 2 small shallots, minced
- ½ cup olive oil
- 2 small endives, thinly sliced
- 2 small watermelon radishes, thinly sliced on a slicer
- 2 tablespoons lemon juice
- 2 teaspoons Dijon mustard
- Salt to taste
- Freshly ground pepper to taste
- 4 tablespoons bacon fat

Directions:

1. Follow the instructions given in the manual and fill the sous vide water oven. Preheat it to 145°F.
2. Place the eggs on a spoon, one at a time, and gently lower them in the water bath and place on the rack. Set the timer for 60 minutes.
3. Meanwhile, place a large skillet over medium heat. Add bacon and cook until golden brown, then turn off the heat.
4. Remove bacon and place on a plate.
5. Use 4 tablespoons of fat from the pan for the dressing.
6. To make dressing: Add all the ingredients for dressing, except oil and bacon fat, into a bowl and whisk until well combined.
7. Pour olive oil and bacon fat in a drizzle, whisking simultaneously. Keep whisking until the

dressing is emulsified.
8. To assemble: Toss all the vegetables into a large bowl.
9. Add bacon and toss again, then drizzle the dressing on top and toss well.
10. Serve in bowls. Crack an egg into each bowl. Sprinkle salt and pepper over the eggs and serve.

Shrimp Salad

Serves: 8

Ingredients:

For shrimp:

- 2 pounds shrimp, shelled and deveined
- Salt to taste
- Pepper to taste
- 2 tablespoons paprika

For salad:

- 4 cups cooked corn kernels
- 24 halved cherry tomatoes,
- 2 tablespoons white wine vinegar
- 2 mangoes, peeled, pitted, cubed
- 1 cup torn red lettuce
- 1 cup torn green lettuce
- ½ cup chopped fresh basil
- 3 tablespoons habanero mango hot sauce, or any other hot sauce of your choice
- 4 tablespoons olive oil
- Salt to taste
- Pepper to taste
- 2 tablespoons grated lemon zest

Directions:

1. Follow the instructions given in the manual and fill the sous vide water oven. Preheat to 122°F for sushi grade, or 132°F for well cooked.
2. Sprinkle salt, pepper, and paprika over the shrimp. Place shrimp into a vacuum-seal pouch or Ziploc bag.
3. Vacuum seal the pouch.
4. Submerge the pouch in the water bath and set the timer for 15 to 30 minutes, depending on the desired doneness.
5. For salad: Divide the lettuce leaves into 8 serving bowls. Set aside the cherry tomatoes and add rest of the salad ingredients into a bowl and toss well.
6. Divide mixture among the salad bowls and place over the lettuce. Divide the tomatoes equally and place over the salad.
7. Remove the shrimp from the pouch. Dry the shrimp by patting with paper towels.
8. Place a non-stick pan over medium-high heat. Add shrimp and cook until light brown.
9. Divide the shrimp into the salad bowls and place on the tomatoes. Sprinkle basil and lemon zest and serve.

Waldorf Chicken Salad

Serves: 4

Ingredients:

- 4 chicken breasts, boneless, skinless
- 2 teaspoons extra virgin olive oil
- 2 cups halved seedless red grapes
- Juice of a lemon
- 2/3 cup mayonnaise
- 1 teaspoon Dijon mustard
- Salt to taste
- Freshly ground pepper to taste
- 2 cups chopped, walnuts, toasted
- 2 small apples, cored, diced
- 4 ribs celery, chopped
- 2 teaspoons red wine vinegar

Directions:

1. Follow the instructions given in the manual and fill the sous vide water oven. Preheat it to 140°F.
2. Sprinkle salt and pepper all over the chicken and place in a large Ziploc or vacuum-seal pouch. Use 2, if required. Add olive oil. Vacuum seal the pouch.
3. Submerge the pouch in water bath and adjust the timer for 2 hours or until cooked through.
4. Just before the timer goes off, prepare an ice water bath by filling a large bowl with water and ice.
5. When done, remove the pouch from the water bath and immerse in the ice water bath. Once the chicken has cooled, remove the pouch from the water bath.
6. Chop the chicken into bite-sized pieces.
7. Place apples in a bowl and drizzle with lemon juice. Toss well.
8. For dressing: Add mustard, mayonnaise, salt, pepper, and red wine vinegar into a bowl and whisk well.
9. Add chicken, walnuts, celery, and grapes into a large bowl. Toss well and add the dressing.
10. Fold until well combined.
11. Serve over a bed of salad greens or in sandwiches.

Chicken Caesar Salad

Serves: 4

Ingredients:

- 4 chicken breasts
- 1 cup grated parmesan cheese
- 2 heads romaine lettuce, chopped
- Croutons (optional)
- Caesar dressing, as required
- Salt to taste
- Pepper to taste

Directions:

1. Follow the instructions given in the manual and fill the sous vide water oven. Preheat it to 140°F.
2. Sprinkle salt and pepper all over the chicken and place in a large Ziploc or vacuum-seal pouch. Use 2, if required. Add olive oil and vacuum seal the pouch.
3. Submerge the pouch in water bath and adjust the timer for 2 hours, or until cooked through.
4. Just before the timer goes off, make an ice water bath by filling a large bowl with water and ice.
5. When done, remove the pouch from the water bath and immerse in the ice water bath. When cooled, remove the pouch from the water bath.
6. Chop the chicken into bite-sized pieces. Place in a bowl. Also add lettuce, cheese, croutons and caesar dressing and fold gently.
7. Serve.

Salad Lyonnaise

Serves: 8

Ingredients:

- 8 large eggs
- 4 tablespoons sherry vinegar
- ½ cup extra-virgin olive oil
- 4 tablespoons grainy mustard
- 2 tablespoons honey
- 4 heads frisée lettuce
- 16 ounces bacon, cut into ½ inch thick strips
- Salt to taste
- Freshly ground pepper to taste

Directions:

1. Follow the instructions given in the manual and fill the sous vide water oven. Preheat it to 147°F.
2. Place the eggs on a spoon, one at a time, and gently lower them into the water bath and place on the rack. Set the timer for 45 minutes.
3. Remove the eggs from the water bath. When cool enough to handle, peel the eggs. Cut into quarters.
4. Meanwhile, place a large skillet over medium heat. Add bacon and cook until golden brown, then turn off the heat.
5. Place bacon on a plate lined with paper towels.
6. To make dressing: Add oil, vinegar, mustard, honey, salt and pepper into a bowl and whisk well.
7. Place frisée in a bowl. Pour dressing over the lettuce and toss well.
8. Place on plates, with 4 pieces of egg on each plate. Sprinkle with salt and pepper.
9. Top with bacon and serve.

Garden Vegetable Salad

Serves: 8

Ingredients:

For the sous vide vegetables:

- 16 French breakfast radishes or red radishes, quartered lengthwise
- 16 baby pattypan squash, quartered lengthwise
- 4 whole carrots, peeled, sliced into 3-inch pieces
- 16 baby zucchini, quartered lengthwise
- 24 sugar snap peas, trimmed, discard strings
- 16 slices English cucumber, peeled
- 16 baby turnips, peeled, sliced in half
- 16 haricot verts or yellow wax beans
- 16 whole red pearl onions, peeled, halved
- 16 baby golden baby beets, peeled, quartered
- 10 tablespoons extra-virgin olive oil
- 6 tablespoons kosher salt or to taste

For the salad:

- 16 ounce fresh chèvre
- 20 fresh basil leaves, finely chopped
- 20 fresh mint leaves, finely chopped
- 6 tablespoons chives, finely chopped
- 20 fresh Italian parsley leaves, finely chopped
- 6 tablespoons olive oil
- 2 tablespoons kosher salt
- 8 tablespoons pistachio, toasted, ground
- 2 bunches watercress
- 2 bunches baby romaine
- ½ bunch arugula
- Extra olive oil to drizzle
- Fresh herbs of your choice to garnish
- Juice of a lemon

Directions:

1. Follow the instructions given in the manual and fill the sous vide water oven. Preheat it to 156°F.
2. For sous vide vegetables: Place each vegetable in a different pouch and drizzle a tablespoon of oil in each. Season with salt.
3. Vacuum seal the pouches.

4. Submerge the pouches in water bath and adjust the timer for 2 hours or until cooked through.
5. Note that cooking time varies for each vegetable. Carrots and beets take 45 minutes to cook, onions and turnips take about 22 minutes to cook, and the rest of the vegetables take 6 to 8 minutes.
6. Fill a large bowl with water and ice. As each vegetable is cooked, pull the pouch out and place in the bowl of chilled water bath for 10 minutes.
7. Meanwhile, in a bowl, mix together the chèvre, herbs, olive oil, salt, and nuts.
8. To serve: Arrange on a large serving platter with watercress and arugula. Layer all the vegetables, except the carrots, over the watercress and arugula.
9. With a peeler, peel the carrots into ribbons and place all over the salad.
10. Drizzle with olive oil and lemon juice.
11. Finally, top with the nut mixture. Sprinkle fresh herbs on top and serve.

Fennel and Orange Quinoa Salad

Serves: 4

Ingredients:

- 7 ounces quinoa
- 2 fennel bulbs, cut into eighths
- A large pinch saffron
- 2 teaspoons toasted sesame seeds
- 6 tablespoons extra-virgin olive oil
- Salt to taste
- 4 cups vegetable stock
- 4 ounces orange juice
- ¼ cup pomegranate seeds
- A handful fresh cilantro, chopped
- 2 tablespoons lemon vinegar
- Freshly ground pepper to taste

For tahini dressing:

- 2 tablespoons tahini
- 3.8 ounces olive oil

For serving:

- A large pinch salt
- 2 tablespoons pine nuts
- Few orange segments, deseeded, chopped
- A handful coriander cress
- Few nasturtium leaves

Directions:

1. For quinoa: Place the saucepan over medium heat and add the quinoa and stock.
2. Once it starts to boil, lower heat and cook it until liquid has been absorbed. Turn the heat off and fluff it with a fork. Allow it to cool.
3. Follow the instructions given in the manual and fill the sous vide water oven. Preheat it to 85°F.
4. Add fennel, saffron, and orange juice into a Ziploc bag or vacuum-seal pouch. Vacuum seal the pouch.
5. Submerge the pouch in water bath and adjust the timer for 20 minutes.
6. Remove the pouch from the water bath. Open the pouch and discard the liquid from inside.
7. Heat a skillet over medium flame, then add fennel and cook until brown. Flip and cook

well on both sides.
8. Add quinoa, pomegranate, and fennel into a large bowl. Toss well.
9. To make lemon dressing: Add lemon vinegar and olive oil into a small bowl and whisk well.
10. Pour over the quinoa. Season with salt and pepper. Toss well.
11. For pine nuts: Place a pan over low heat. When the pan heats, add pine nuts and stir until toasted.
12. Add salt and toss well.
13. To make tahini dressing: Add all the ingredients for tahini dressing into a bowl and whisk well.
14. To assemble: Divide the quinoa into 4 bowls.
15. Top with pine nuts, orange, coriander, cress, and nasturtium leaves. Spoon the tahini dressing on top and serve.

Butternut Squash Salad

Serves: 8

Ingredients:

- 2 medium butternut squashes, trimmed, peeled, deseeded, halved lengthwise, cut into ¾ inch thick slices crosswise
- Kosher salt to taste
- 1 cup balsamic vinegar
- 2 teaspoons Italian seasoning
- 2 large, red pears, peeled, cored, chopped into bite-sized pieces
- 6 tablespoons extra-virgin olive oil
- Freshly ground pepper to taste
- 6 tablespoons honey
- 2 pounds fresh Brussels sprouts, trimmed, thinly sliced

Directions:

1. Follow the instructions given in the manual and fill the sous vide water oven. Preheat it to 194°F.
2. Divide the squash evenly into 2 large vacuum-seal pouches or Ziploc bags. Season with salt and pepper and drizzle with oil. Vacuum seal the pouches.
3. Submerge the pouches in water bath and adjust the timer for 30 minutes.
4. Remove the pouches from the water bath.
5. Meanwhile, add vinegar, Italian seasoning, and honey into a small pan over medium-low heat. Cook until it is 2/3 its original quantity, then turn off the heat.
6. Place Brussels sprouts in a microwave-safe bowl. Place in the microwave and cook for 4 minutes. Drain off any cooked liquid.
7. Add Brussels sprouts, pears, and butternut squash into a large bowl. Toss well.
8. Divide onto plates and spoon the balsamic sauce on top. Season with salt and pepper and serve.

Potato Salad with Creamy Rosemary Garlic Butter Dressing

Serves: 4

Ingredients:

For salad:

- 1 pound red potatoes, cut into 1-inch slices
- 1 sprig of rosemary
- Pepper to taste
- Salt to taste
- 1 ½ tablespoons butter

For creamy rosemary garlic butter dressing:

- 2 tablespoons butter
- ½ teaspoon minced fresh rosemary
- ½ teaspoon salt
- 2 cloves garlic, peeled, minced
- ¼ cup mayonnaise
- Pepper to taste

Directions:

1. Follow the instructions given in the manual and fill the sous vide water oven. Preheat it to 190°F.
2. Add all the ingredients for salad into a Ziploc bag or vacuum-seal pouch. Vacuum seal the pouch.
3. Submerge the pouch in water bath and adjust the timer for 60 minutes.
4. Just before the timer goes off, make an ice water bath by filling a large bowl with water and ice.
5. When done, remove the pouch from the water bath and immerse in the ice water bath. When cooled, remove the pouch from the water bath.
6. For dressing: Place a pot over medium heat and add butter. When butter melts, add garlic and rosemary and sauté for a few seconds until aromatic. Turn off the heat.
7. Transfer into a large bowl. Add mayonnaise, pepper, and salt and mix well.
8. Discard the rosemary sprigs and add the potatoes to the bowl. Stir until well combined.

CHAPTER TEN
SOUS VIDE SOUP RECIPES

Split Lentil Soup with Smoked Ham Hock

Serves: 4

Ingredients:

- 5 cups chicken stock
- 2 smoked ham hocks
- 1 cup finely diced carrot
- 1 cup finely diced celery
- ½ cup finely diced onions
- 2 cups split lentils
- Freshly ground pepper to taste
- Kosher salt to taste
- 2 bay leaves

Directions:

1. Follow the instructions given in the manual and fill the sous vide water oven. Preheat it to 180°F.
2. Add all the ingredients into a large vacuum-seal pouch or Ziploc bag.
3. Vacuum seal the pouch.
4. Submerge the pouch in the water bath. Set the timer for 2 hours.
5. For finishing: Remove the pouch from the water bath and throw out the bay leaves.
6. Take out the ham hock. Remove and discard the bones and fat.
7. Add rest of the ingredients of the pouch into a blender and blend until smooth.

8. Pour into bowls. Divide the meat among the bowls and serve.

Creamy Celery Soup

Serves: 3

Ingredients:

- ½ cup heavy cream
- 2 cups celery, diced roughly
- ½ cup russet potatoes, peeled, diced into small squares
- ½ cup stock (vegetable or chicken)
- ½ cup leek, diced into large pieces
- 1 tablespoon butter
- 1 bay leaf
- 1 teaspoon kosher salt or to taste
- White pepper powder to taste

Directions:
1. Follow the instructions given in the manual and fill the sous vide water oven. Preheat it to 180°F.
2. Toss all ingredients in a Ziploc bag and vacuum seal it. Submerge it in a water bath for about an hour, or until the vegetables are cooked.
3. Once all the ingredients are cooked, take out the bay leaf and puree the rest of the ingredients. Strain the contents through a strainer or sieve discard the remaining solids. Serve hot.

Chicken Ramen

Serves: 4

Ingredients:

- 1 pound chicken thighs, skinless, boneless
- 4 cloves garlic, peeled, minced
- 2 medium onions, chopped
- 4 carrots, peeled, thinly sliced
- 1 medium head Chinese cabbage, shredded
- 2 tablespoons tomato paste
- 8 cups chicken stock
- 2 tablespoons tomato paste
- 4 tablespoons grated fresh ginger
- 4 tablespoons Japanese soy sauce
- 2 tablespoons oil
- 2 tablespoons sugar
- Shichimi togarashi or plain red pepper flakes to taste
- 2 bay leaves
- 2 star anise
- 7 ounces ramen or any other oriental noodles
- 2 scallions, thinly sliced

Directions:

1. Follow the instructions given in the manual and fill the sous vide water oven. Preheat it to 144°F.
2. Place a skillet over medium heat and add oil. When the oil is heated, add onions, garlic, shichimi, and 2 tablespoons ginger. Sauté until the onions are translucent.
3. Add tomato paste and mix well. Remove from heat. Add chicken, carrots, stock, soy sauce, star anise, sugar, and bay leaves. Mix well.
4. Transfer into a large Ziploc bag or vacuum-seal pouch.
5. Submerge the pouch in the water bath and adjust the timer for 8 to 10 hours, or until the chicken is cooked.
6. Remove the chicken from the pouch and, once cool enough to handle, shred the chicken and set it aside. Add rest of the ingredients of the pouch into a pot.
7. Place the pot over medium heat. Add noodles and cabbage and cook until the noodles are al dente.
8. Discard star anise and bay leaves. Add chicken and 2 tablespoons ginger. Heat thoroughly.
9. Serve in bowls. Garnish with green onions and serve.

Chicken and Vegetable Soup

Serves: 8

Ingredients:

- 2 cups zucchini, diced
- 2 cups cauliflower, chopped
- 2 cups red bell pepper, diced
- 8 cups fresh spinach leaves
- 12 baby carrots, chopped
- 2 large onions, chopped
- 2 teaspoons of garlic powder or to taste
- Cayenne pepper to taste
- 4 cups chicken, diced, sous vide cooked
- 8 cups chicken broth
- 2 teaspoons onion powder
- Sea salt to taste
- Black pepper powder to taste
- 2 tablespoons olive oil

Directions:

1. Follow the instructions given in the manual and fill the sous vide water oven. Preheat it to 180°F.
2. Place all the vegetables in a bowl and add all the spices into another bowl. Mix well, then sprinkle the spice mixture over the vegetables. Toss well and transfer into a large Ziploc bag or a vacuum-seal pouch and vacuum seal it. Submerge the pouch in the water bath and adjust the timer for 1 hour, or until the vegetables are cooked.
3. To make the soup: Place a soup pot over medium heat and add oil. When the oil is heated, add broth and let it come to a boil.
4. Lower heat, empty the contents of the pouch into the pot and add chicken and stir. Simmer for 5 to 7 minutes. Turn off the heat.
5. Serve in soup bowls. Serve hot.

Wild Mushroom Bisque

Serves: 8

Ingredients:

- 2 pounds assorted wild mushrooms of your choice
- 2 shallots, thinly sliced
- 4 tablespoons brandy or cognac
- Salt to taste
- Freshly ground pepper to taste
- 1 cup heavy cream
- 6 tablespoons unsalted butter
- 2 tablespoons minced, fresh thyme
- 2 cloves garlic, peeled, minced
- 4 cups water
- Olive oil, to drizzle (optional)

Directions:

1. Follow the instructions given in the manual and fill the sous vide water oven. Preheat it to 190°F.
2. Add all the ingredients into a large vacuum-seal pouch or Ziploc bag.
3. Vacuum seal the pouch.
4. Submerge the pouch in the water bath. Set the timer for 1 hour.
5. When the timer goes off, remove pouch from the water bath. Transfer into a blender and blend until smooth.
6. Serve in bowls. Trickle oil on top, if using, and serve.

Tomato Soup

Serves: 5 to 7
Ingredients:

- 1 can whole or diced tomatoes, peeled
- 1 small fresh tomato, chopped
- 1 small green pepper, chopped
- 1 tablespoon flour
- A pinch cayenne pepper
- 1 tablespoon dried basil leaves
- ¼ cup heavy cream
- ¼ cup butter
- 1 cup milk
- 1 clove garlic, chopped
- Salt and pepper, as needed

Direction:

1. Heat a saucepan over medium flame and melt half the butter. Add the flour and sauté for a couple of minutes until it becomes brown. Make sure you stir it constantly.
2. Add the milk and continue stirring until the mixture starts bubbling and thickens.
3. Pour the cream and stir again for a minute. Don't let it boil—once it's warm enough, take it off the heat and set aside.
4. Heat another saucepan over medium flame. Melt the rest of the butter and add onions, garlic, and green pepper. Sauté for 3 to 4 minutes.
5. Add diced tomatoes, chopped tomato, and basil and mix well.
6. Reduce the heat and add cayenne pepper, white sauce, salt and pepper.
7. Follow the instructions given in the manual and fill the sous vide water oven. Preheat it to 175°F.
8. Transfer the vegetables to a Ziploc bag and vacuum seal it. Submerge the pouch in the water bath for 45 minutes.
9. When cooked, puree the soup and serve hot.

Beet Soup with Caraway and Yogurt

Serves: 8

Ingredients:

- 2 tablespoons extra-virgin olive oil
- 2 medium onions, chopped
- Salt to taste
- 2 bay leaves
- 1 cup whole milk yogurt + extra to serve
- Fresh dill fronds, to serve
- 3 teaspoons caraway seeds
- 2 leeks, halved, thinly sliced
- 4 pounds beets, peeled, chopped
- 6 cups chicken broth or water
- 1 tablespoon apple cider vinegar or to taste

Directions:

1. Follow the instructions given in the manual and fill the sous vide water oven. Preheat it to 185°F.
2. Place a skillet over medium flame and add oil. When the oil is heated, add caraway seeds. When they crackle, add leeks, onion and a bit of salt and cook until tender. Turn off the heat.
3. Add beets, about a teaspoon of salt, and bay leaves and mix well. Transfer into 2 large vacuum-seal pouches or Ziploc bags.
4. Vacuum seal the pouches.
5. Submerge the pouches in the water bath. Set the timer for 2 hours.
6. When the timer goes off, remove pouch from the water bath. Transfer into a blender. Add some broth and blend until smooth.
7. Pour into a saucepan. Add yogurt, vinegar, and salt to taste. Mix well.
8. Serve in bowls and drizzle some yogurt on top. Place dill fronds in each bowl and serve.

Sweet Corn and Green Chili Soup

Serves: 8

Ingredients:

- 2 bags frozen sweet corn
- 6 bulbs roasted garlic, peeled
- 2 cups chicken stock
- 1 medium onion, sautéed to golden brown
- Salt to taste
- Pepper to taste
- 2 large whole green chilies, char the skin using a culinary torch, deseed if desired

Directions:

1. Follow the instructions given in the manual and fill the sous vide water oven. Preheat it to 83°F.
2. Add all the ingredients except green chilies into a large vacuum-seal pouch or Ziploc bag.
3. Vacuum seal the pouch.
4. Submerge the pouch in the water bath. Set the timer for 1½ hours or until cooked.
5. When the timer goes off, remove pouch from the water bath. Transfer into a blender. Add the green chilies and blend until smooth.
6. Strain the soup if desired. Taste and adjust the seasonings if required.
7. Serve in bowls.

Tri Tip Chili

Serves: 8

Ingredients:

- 4 pounds tri tip roast
- 2 onions, diced
- 2 cans (15 ounces each) petite diced tomatoes, with its juices
- 4 tablespoons tomato paste
- 16 ounces tomato sauce (refer to chapter on sauces for the recipe)
- 3 cups beef broth
- 2 tablespoons olive oil
- 2 cans (15.5 ounces each) red kidney beans, drained, rinsed
- 4 tablespoons ground cumin
- 2 tablespoons garlic powder
- 1 teaspoon pepper, or to taste
- 5 tablespoons chili powder, or to taste
- 3 tablespoons sugar
- 2 teaspoons salt, or to taste
- ½ teaspoon cayenne pepper

To serve:

- Sour cream
- Grated cheddar cheese

Directions:

1. Follow the instructions given in the manual and fill the sous vide water oven. Preheat it to 131°F.
2. Sprinkle salt over the tri tip and place in a large vacuum bag. Vacuum seal the pouch.
3. Submerge the pouch in the water bath. Set the timer for 3 hours or until cooked.
4. When the timer goes off, remove pouch from the water bath. Remove the tri tip from the pouch and dry by patting with paper towels.
5. Place a large skillet over high heat. Add oil and let it heat.
6. Sprinkle salt and pepper over the meat and place in the pan. Cook for a couple of minutes. Flip and cook well on the other side, too.
7. Remove meat and, when it is cool enough to handle, cut into bite-sized pieces. Set it aside.
8. To make chili: Place a large soup pot over medium heat and add oil. When the oil is heated, onions and sauté until translucent.
9. Add all the spices, sugar, and tomato paste and stir for a few seconds until aromatic.
10. Stir in broth, beans, tomatoes, and tomato sauce. When it begins to boil, reduce the heat and simmer for about 30 minutes. Stir every 10 minutes. Turn off the heat.
11. Cover the pot. Let the chili sit for 10 minutes. Add the tri tip meat into the pot and stir.

12. Serve in bowls. Garnish with cheddar cheese and sour cream.

Borscht

Serves: 4

Ingredients:

- 2 large beetroots, peeled, sliced
- 1 medium onion, peeled, sliced
- ¼ head red cabbage, thinly sliced
- ½ cup chopped dill + extra to serve
- Salt to taste
- Pepper to taste
- 2 large carrots, peeled, sliced
- 1 medium russet potato, peeled, sliced
- 4 cups vegetable broth or beef broth
- 1 ½ tablespoons red wine vinegar
- ½ cup sour cream, to serve

Directions:

1. Follow the instructions given in the manual and fill the sous vide water oven. Preheat it to 83°F.
2. Add carrots, beets, potato, and onions in a single into a large vacuum-seal pouch or Ziploc bag.
3. Add cabbage in another pouch.
4. Vacuum seal the pouches.
5. Submerge the pouches in the water bath. Set the timer for 1½ hours or until vegetables are cooked.
6. When the timer goes off, remove pouches from the water bath. Transfer the contents of beets pouch into a blender and blend until smooth.
7. Taste and adjust the seasonings if required.
8. Place a soup pot over high heat and let it come to a boil. Add blended soup, cabbage, vinegar, salt, pepper, and dill. Stir well and lower heat to low heat. Let it simmer for a few minutes.
9. Dish into bowls and drizzle with sour cream. Sprinkle dill on top and serve.

Beef Bourguignon

Serves: 8

Ingredients:

- 2 tablespoons extra-virgin olive oil
- 3 pounds beef chuck roast, cut into 1-inch pieces
- 3 teaspoons kosher salt, divided
- 4 carrots, quartered lengthwise, cut into 1-inch pieces
- 4 cloves garlic, peeled, minced
- 2 cups water
- 2 tablespoons tomato paste
- 2 bay leaves
- 20 ounces cremini mushrooms, thinly sliced
- 12 ounces bacon, thinly sliced into lardons
- 4 tablespoons cornstarch
- 1 teaspoon freshly ground pepper
- 2 onions, sliced
- 2 bottles dry red wine
- 2 tablespoons beef bouillon
- 2 teaspoons minced fresh thyme leaves
- 8 tablespoons unsalted butter, at room temperature, divided
- 4 tablespoons all-purpose flour

Directions:

1. Follow the instructions given in the manual and fill the sous vide water oven. Preheat it to 140°F.
2. Place a large skillet over medium heat and add oil. When the oil is heated, add bacon and cook until crisp. Remove bacon and place in a large Ziploc bag or vacuum-seal pouch.
3. Dry the beef with paper towels. Sprinkle cornstarch, pepper, and 2 teaspoons salt over the beef. Toss well.
4. Place a large pan over medium heat. Add a little of the oil. When the oil is heated, add some of the beef and cook until brown all over. Cook the remaining beef in batches, using a little of the oil with each batch.
5. Remove with a slotted spoon and place in the pouch along with bacon.
6. Add onions, carrot, and 1 teaspoon salt into the same skillet. Sauté until onions turn light brown.
7. Stir in the garlic and cook until aromatic. Turn off the heat and add the vegetables into the pouch with beef. Drain off any fat remaining in the pan.
8. Pour wine into the skillet.
9. Stir in water and beef bouillon. Cook until the liquid in the pan is reduced to ¼ its original quantity.
10. Pour into the pouch. Also add the tomato paste, bay leaves, and thyme.
11. Vacuum seal the pouch.
12. Submerge the pouch in the water bath. Set the timer for 16 to 24 hours. Use plastic wrap to cover the water bath. This helps to reduce water evaporation.

13. During the last 5 minutes of cooking, place a large skillet over medium heat and add 4 tablespoons butter. When butter melts, add mushrooms and cook until soft.
14. Remove the pouch from the water bath. Snip off a corner of the bag and add the liquid from the bag into the skillet.
15. Add 4 tablespoons butter and flour into a bowl and mix well. Add into the skillet. Increase the heat to medium-high and stir often until the sauce thickens.
16. Add meat and vegetables from the pouch into the skillet. Mix well.
17. Turn off the heat. Place in a serving bowl and sprinkle with thyme.
18. Serve with roasted potatoes or bread or mashed cauliflower, if desired.

Beef Burgundy Stew

Serves: 12

Ingredients:

- 6 slices thick-cut bacon, cut into ¼-inch strips
- 4 pounds sirloin roast, cut into 1-inch cubes
- 2 medium onions, thinly sliced
- 4 cups dry red wine
- 2 tablespoons tomato paste
- 2 cloves garlic, minced
- 2 bay leaves
- 14 ounces frozen pearl onions, thawed
- 4 tablespoons unsalted butter
- 4 carrots, peeled, cut into ¼-inch thick slices
- 6 tablespoons flour
- 3 cups beef stock
- 2 tablespoons Worcestershire sauce
- 2 teaspoons dried thyme
- 20 ounces white mushrooms, cleaned, quartered
- A handful fresh parsley, chopped, to garnish

Directions:

1. Follow the instructions given in the manual and fill the sous vide water oven. Preheat it to 140°F.
2. Place a large heavy-bottomed skillet over medium-high heat. When the pan is warm, add bacon and cook until crisp. Remove bacon and place on a plate lined with paper towels.
3. Retain about 2 tablespoons of the bacon fat (released in the pan while cooking) and discard the rest.
4. Dry the meat cubes with paper towels.
5. Add 2 tablespoons butter into the skillet. When butter melts, add meat in a single layer and cook until brown all over. Cook in batches if required.
6. Stir in the carrots and onion and cook until slightly tender.
7. Sprinkle flour on top and mix until the meat and vegetables are well coated.
8. Pour wine into the skillet, then stir in 2 cups stock, Worcestershire sauce, bay leaves, tomato paste, garlic and thyme and mix well.
9. When it begins to boil, lower heat and cook until slightly thick. Turn off the heat.
10. Transfer into 1 or 2 large vacuum-seal pouches or Ziploc bags. Vacuum seal the pouches.
11. Submerge the pouch in the water bath. Adjust the timer for 6 hours.
12. During the last 30 minutes of cooking, place a skillet over medium heat and add 2 tablespoons butter. When butter melts, add mushroom and pearl onions and cook until dry.

13. Stir in rest of the stock and cook until dry. Remove the mushrooms into a large bowl.
14. To finish: Place a fine wire mesh strainer over a bowl. Empty the pouch into the strainer and add the solids into the bowl of mushrooms.
15. Pour the strained liquid into a skillet. Place the skillet over medium flame and let it come to a boil. Discard any scum and fat that is floating on top. Reduce the heat and simmer until slightly thick.
16. Stir in the meat and mushroom mixture. Mix well. Heat thoroughly. Transfer into a bowl.
17. Sprinkle parsley on top and serve.

CHAPTER ELEVEN
SNACK RECIPES

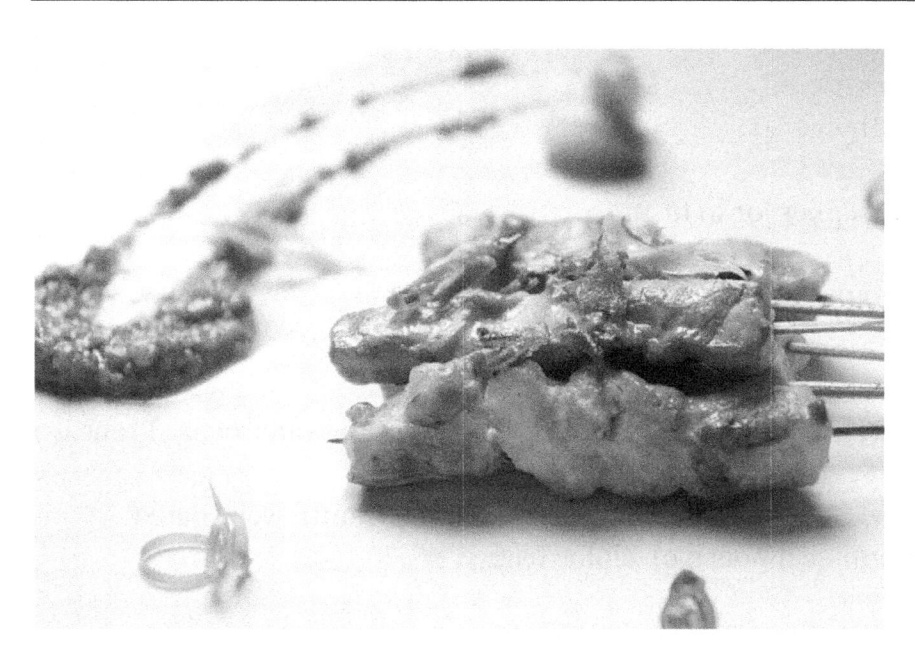

Citrus Yogurt

Serves: 8

Ingredients:

- 1 cup yogurt
- 8 cups full cream milk
- 1 tablespoon grated orange zest
- 1 tablespoon grated lime zest
- 1 tablespoon grated lemon zest

Directions:

1. Follow the instructions given in the manual and fill the sous vide water oven. Preheat it to 113°F.
2. Pour milk into a saucepan and place over medium heat. When the temperature of the milk reaches 180°F, turn off the heat. Let the milk cool to 110°F.
3. Add 2 tablespoons of yogurt in each of 8 canning jars. Divide the milk among the jars, then divide the zests among the jars and stir. Fasten the lid on the jars.
4. Immerse the filled jars in the water bath. The lids of the jars should be above the level of water in the cooker.
5. Set the timer for 3 hours.
6. Remove from the water bath and cool completely. Refrigerate for a few hours before use.

Sous Vide Mushrooms

Serves: 8

Ingredients:

- 2 pounds mushrooms of your choice
- 4 tablespoons extra-virgin olive oil
- 4 teaspoons minced fresh thyme
- 1 teaspoon salt or to taste
- 1 teaspoon freshly ground pepper, or to taste
- 4 tablespoons soy sauce
- 2 tablespoons vinegar of your choice

Directions:

1. Follow the instructions given in the manual and fill the sous vide water oven. Preheat it to 176°F.
2. Place mushrooms in a bowl. Add rest of the ingredients and stir until well coated.
3. Transfer into a large vacuum-seal pouch or Ziploc bag.
4. Vacuum seal the pouch.
5. Submerge the pouch in the water bath. Set the timer for 30 minutes.
6. When the timer goes off, remove pouch from the water bath. Set aside to cool.
7. Open the pouch and transfer into a bowl.
8. Serve right away.

Sous Vide Corn

Serves: 2

Ingredients:

- 2 ears corn
- Kosher salt to taste
- 1 tablespoon butter + extra to serve

Aromatics: (optional, to taste)

- Handful cilantro, chopped
- 1 or 2 scallions, chopped
- Dried red chilies to taste
- 4 or 5 cloves garlic, minced

Directions:

1. Follow the instructions given in the manual and fill the sous vide water oven. Preheat it to 183°F.
2. Add all the ingredients including the aromatics into a vacuum-seal pouch or Ziploc bag. Vacuum seal the pouch.
3. Submerge the pouch in the water bath and fix on the edge of the water bath with clips.
4. Set timer for 30 minutes.
5. Remove corn from the pouch and discard the rest of the ingredients.
6. Brush with more butter and serve.

Meatballs

Serves: 8 to 10

Ingredients:

- 2 pounds ground beef
- 4 to 6 ounces milk
- ½ teaspoon pepper
- 1 shallot minced
- 2 tablespoons dried oregano
- 6 tablespoons grated parmesan cheese
- ½ cup dried breadcrumbs
- 1 teaspoon salt, or to taste
- 2 large eggs, beaten
- 1/3 cup chopped parsley
- 2 tablespoons garlic powder
- Dip of your choice, to serve
- A little oil to seas (optional)

Directions:

1. Add all the ingredients into a large bowl and mix with your hands until just incorporated. Do not mix for long, as the meat will tend to get tough.
2. Make 1-inch balls of the mixture. Place on a tray and freeze until firm.
3. Follow the instructions given in the manual and fill the sous vide water oven. Preheat it to 135°F.
4. Transfer the meatballs into 1 or 2 large vacuum-seal pouches or Ziploc bags.
5. Vacuum seal the pouches.
6. Immerse the pouches in the water bath. Set the timer for 3 hours.
7. When the timer goes off, remove pouch from the water bath. Set aside to cool.
8. Open the pouch and transfer into a bowl.
9. Serve with a dip of your choice.
10. If you want to sear the meatballs: Place a non-stick pan over medium heat and add a bit of oil. When the oil is heated, add meatballs and cook until browned.
11. Serve.

Szechuan Pork Belly Bites with BBQ Glaze

Serves: 8 to 10

Ingredients:

- 2½ pounds pork belly strips, discard rind, let the fat remain, cut into 1-inch pieces
- White pepper to taste
- 2 star anise pods
- 2 tablespoons honey
- Peel of 2 clementines

To finish:

- 4 tablespoons Szechuan peppercorns, ground
- BBQ sauce, as required
- Salt to taste

Directions:

1. Follow the instructions given in the manual and fill the sous vide water oven. Preheat it to 185°F.
2. Place pork in a bowl. Add honey, clementines, star anise, and pepper and stir.
3. Transfer into a large vacuum-seal pouch or Ziploc bag.
4. Vacuum seal the pouch.
5. Submerge the pouch in the water bath. Set the timer for 6 to 10 hours.
6. When the timer goes off, remove pouch from the water bath. Set aside to cool.
7. Open the pouch and drain off the liquid.
8. To finish: Dry the pork pieces with paper towels.
9. Add Szechuan peppercorns and salt into a bowl and stir.
10. Dredge the fat part of the pork pieces in the Szechuan mixture and place on a lined baking sheet.
11. Brush some BBQ sauce over the pork pieces.
12. Bake in a preheated oven at 350°F for 5 to 6 minutes.
13. Insert toothpicks on the pork pieces and serve with some BBQ sauce.

Chicken Satay

Serves: 6 to 8

Ingredients:

- ½ cup satay sauce, divided + extra for dipping
- 2 large chicken breasts, cut into bite-sized pieces

Directions:

1. In a bowl, mix together chicken pieces and ½ the marinade. Set aside for a minimum of 2 to 3 hours.
2. Follow the instructions given in the manual and fill the sous vide water oven. Preheat it to 140°F.
3. Place the chicken pieces in a large Ziploc bag. Vacuum seal the pouch.
4. Submerge the pouch in water bath and adjust the timer for 85 minutes.
5. To finish: Remove the bag from the water bath. Open the pouch and thread the chicken onto skewers.
6. Set an oven to broil mode and preheat. Place the skewers in the oven and broil for a few minutes until golden brown in color.
7. Transfer onto a serving platter. Insert toothpicks in the chicken pieces.
8. Serve with satay sauce.

Tomato Sushi

Serves: 24

Ingredients:

For tomatoes:

- 6 Roma tomatoes
- 2 tablespoons soy sauce
- 2 cups water
- 6 nori sheets
- ½ teaspoon salt

For sushi rice:

- 2 cups uncooked glutinous white rice, rinsed
- ½ cup rice vinegar
- ½ teaspoon salt
- 3 cups water
- 4 tablespoons sugar

Directions:

1. For tomatoes: Follow the instructions given in the manual and fill the sous vide water oven. Preheat it to 140°F.
2. Add 4 nori sheets, soy sauce, water, and salt in a large saucepan over medium heat.
3. Simmer until it has reduced to half its original quantity. Turn off the heat.
4. Cut off a slice from the top of the tomatoes. Make cuts in the shape of an "X" with a paring knife.
5. Place a pan with water over high heat. When it begins to boil, add the tomatoes and let it cook for about 30 to 60 seconds. Remove the tomatoes and place in a bowl filled with ice and water.
6. Peel the tomatoes. Cut each into quarters. Discard the seeds.
7. Place the tomatoes in the nori water. Transfer into a vacuum-seal pouch or Ziploc bag. Vacuum seal the pouch.
8. Submerge the pouch in water bath and adjust the timer for 4 hours.
9. To make sushi rice: Add vinegar, salt, and sugar into a saucepan over medium heat. Stir frequently until sugar dissolves. Turn off the heat.
10. Add rice and water into a pot over high heat. When it begins to boil, reduce the heat and cover with a lid. Simmer until all liquid is absorbed.
11. Add sugar solution and mix well. Turn off the heat.
12. To assemble: Cut the remaining nori sheets into 24 strips. Remove the pouch from the water bath.
13. When the rice is cool enough to handle, divide the rice into 24 equal portions and shape

into sushi.
14. Place a piece of tomato on each sushi. Wrap the sushi along with the tomato with a nori strip and place on a serving platter.
15. Serve.

Lemon-Butter Shrimp

Serves: 8

Ingredients:

- 2 pounds large shrimp, peeled, deveined
- 16 strips (½ inch each) lemon zest
- 4 ounces chilled butter, cut into 8 slices
- 1 teaspoon creole seasoning or to taste + extra to serve
- 6 sprigs fresh thyme

Directions:

1. Follow the instructions given in the manual and fill the sous vide water oven. Preheat it to 135°F.
2. Place shrimp in a bowl. Sprinkle creole seasoning on top and toss well.
3. Transfer into a large Ziploc bag or vacuum-seal pouch. Spread the shrimp in a single layer. Use 2 pouches, if required.
4. Scatter lemon zest, butter, and thyme all over the shrimp. Vacuum seal the pouch.
5. Submerge the pouch in water bath and adjust the timer for 30 minutes.
6. When the timer goes off, remove the pouch from the water bath.
7. Transfer the shrimp onto a serving platter. Sprinkle some more creole seasoning on top and serve.

Fresh Vegetables Confit

Serves: 8 to 10

Ingredients:

- 1 cup peeled pearl onions
- 1 cup peeled garlic cloves
- 6 cups olive oil
- 2 cups halved, deseeded mini peppers

To serve:

- 10 to 12 ounces spreadable goat cheese
- Ciabatta bread slices, as required, toasted
- Salt to taste
- Fresh herbs of your choice, chopped to garnish

Directions:

1. Follow the instructions given in the manual and fill the sous vide water oven. Preheat it to 185°F.
2. Place garlic a Ziploc bag or vacuum-seal pouch. Pour 1½ cups oil into the pouch.
3. Add mini peppers into a second Ziploc bag. Pour 3 cups oil into the pouch.
4. Add pearl onions into a third Ziploc bag. Pour 1½ cups oil into the pouch.
5. Vacuum seal the pouches.
6. Immerse the pouches in water bath and adjust the timer for 1½ hours. When the timer goes off, remove the pouches from the water bath and place in chilled water for 30 minutes.
7. Spread goat cheese over toasted ciabatta slices. Top with vegetables from each pouch. Garnish with fresh herbs and serve.

Escargot Sous Vide

Serves: 8

Ingredients:

For snails:

- 48 large canned French helix snails with shells
- 4 medium carrots, peeled, diced
- 2 bay leaves
- Pepper to taste
- Coarse salt to taste
- 4 sprigs thyme, use only leaves
- 3 cups mushroom stock, frozen
- 2 medium onions, diced

To serve:

- 1 stick butter
- 2 tablespoons minced, roasted garlic from jar
- ½ cup very dry white wine
- 2 tablespoons finely minced shallot
- ½ teaspoon sea salt
- ¼ cup finely chopped parsley
- Crusty bread

Directions:

1. Follow the instructions given in the manual and fill the sous vide water oven. Preheat it to 154°F.
2. Take a bowl of water and soak the snails in it. Remove the stomach and intestines. Set aside the shells.
3. Add all the ingredients including the snails in a large vacuum-seal pouch.
4. Vacuum seal the pouch.
5. Submerge the pouch in water bath and adjust the timer for 5 to 6 hours.
6. When the timer goes off, remove the pouch from the water bath.
7. Open the pouch and pour the cooked juices into a bowl. Set it aside.
8. Remove the snails and set aside. Throw away the vegetables.
9. For finishing: Place a non-stick pan over medium heat and add butter. When butter melts, add garlic and shallots and sauté until soft.
10. Pour wine. Scrape the bottom of the pan to remove any browned bits.
11. Add snails and parsley and mix well. Heat thoroughly.
12. Turn off the heat. Remove the snails from the pan and place it back in its shell.
13. Place snails on a serving platter. Spoon the butter/wine mixture from the pan over the

snails, in each shell.
14. Serve with crusty bread.

CHAPTER TWELVE
SOUS VIDE MAIN COURSE RECIPES

Sesame Chicken

Serves: 2 or 3

Ingredients:

For chicken:

- ¾ pound chicken breast, cut into 1-inch cubes
- 1 clove garlic, smashed
- ½ tablespoon soy sauce
- ½ inch fresh ginger, thinly sliced
- ½ tablespoon sesame oil
- ½ tablespoon rice wine vinegar

For sesame sauce:

- 2 tablespoons soy sauce
- 3 tablespoons honey
- 3 tablespoons chicken stock or water
- 1 teaspoon sesame oil
- ½ tablespoon sesame seeds + extra to garnish
- 2 tablespoons rice wine vinegar
- ½ tablespoon cornstarch

- ½ teaspoon chili garlic sauce (optional)
- 1 scallion, thinly sliced, to garnish
- Cooked white rice to serve

Directions:

1. Follow the instructions given in the manual and fill the sous vide water oven. Preheat it to 158°F.
2. Add all the ingredients for chicken into a bowl and stir. Transfer into a Ziploc bag or vacuum-seal pouch.
3. Spread the chicken in a single layer. Vacuum seal the pouch.
4. Submerge the pouch in water bath and adjust the timer for 2 hours.
5. When the timer goes off, remove the pouch from the water bath.
6. To make sauce: Add all the ingredients for sauce into a skillet and place over medium flame. Stir frequently until thick.
7. Add only chicken from the pouch into the skillet. Discard the remaining ingredients from the pouch.
8. Mix the chicken well with the sauce. Heat thoroughly.
9. Serve rice in individual serving plates and spoon the chicken over the rice. Garnish with sesame seeds and scallions and serve.

Sous Vide Buffalo Chicken Lettuce Wraps

Serves: 4 or 5

Ingredients:

- 1 ½ pounds chicken breast
- ½ tablespoon honey
- ½ teaspoon green scotch bonnet pepper sauce
- Salt to taste
- Pepper to taste
- 4 tablespoons buffalo sauce
- ½ tablespoon chili-lime Cholula
- 2 cloves garlic, minced

To finish:

- 4 or 5 large lettuce leaves
- 1 carrot, shredded
- Blue cheese dressing or ranch dressing, to drizzle
- ½ cup grated gorgonzola cheese
- 1 celery stalk, thinly sliced
- 4 tablespoons buffalo sauce
- ½ tablespoon butter
- 1 teaspoon lime juice, or to taste

Directions:

1. Follow the instructions given in the manual and fill the sous vide water oven. Preheat it to 150°F.
2. Sprinkle salt and pepper all over the chicken and place in a large Ziploc or vacuum-seal pouch. Use 2 pouches, if required. Add rest of the ingredients for chicken into a bowl and whisk well. Pour into the pouch and all over the chicken. Move the pouch in between your hands to mix the sauce with the chicken. Vacuum seal the pouch.
3. Submerge the pouch in water bath and adjust the timer for 1 hour or until cooked through.
4. Remove the pouch from the water bath. Remove the chicken and place on your cutting board. Retain the remaining ingredients in the pouch.
5. Chop or shred the chicken into bite-sized pieces.
6. To finish: Place a skillet over medium heat and add butter. When the butter melts, add the retained cooked liquid (from the pouch) into the skillet. Add lime juice and buffalo sauce. When it begins to boil, reduce the heat and simmer until slightly thick.
7. Add chicken and mix well.
8. To serve: Place the lettuce leaves on a platter. Place ½ cup chicken on each lettuce leaf. Divide the carrots, cheese, and celery among the leaves.
9. Drizzle the dressing on top and serve.

Succulent Sous Vide Chicken with Chili, Ginger and Spring Onion

Serves: 2

Ingredients:

- 2 chicken breasts
- 2 tablespoons honey
- 10 ginger matchsticks,
- ¼ green chili, deseeded, thinly sliced
- 8 chunks pineapple
- 2 star anise
- 2 teaspoons coriander seeds
- 2 tablespoons light soy sauce
- 1 spring onion, cut into 2-cm pieces along the diagonal
- ¼ red chili, deseeded, sliced
- 2 tablespoons sesame seeds
- Fresh cilantro, chopped, to garnish

Directions:

1. Follow the instructions given in the manual and fill the sous vide water oven. Preheat it to 150°F.
2. Divide all the ingredients equally into 2 vacuum-seal pouches or Ziploc bags. Vacuum seal the pouches.
3. Submerge the pouches in the water bath. Set the timer for 40 minutes or until cooked. Do not stack the pouches.
4. If using right away, place a pan over medium heat. Remove the chicken from the pouches and place in the pan. Cook until golden brown. Add spring onions and empty the remaining ingredients from the pouches into the pan. Taste and adjust the honey and soy sauce if required.
5. If using later. Place the bags in chilled water until completely cold. Refrigerate until use, for up to 48 hours. Place in a water bath for 30 minutes and follow the previous step.

Spicy Chicken with Smoked Paprika Spice Rub

Serves: 2

Ingredients:

- ½ cup water
- 2 ½ teaspoons granulated sugar
- 2 teaspoons unsalted butter, softened
- ¼ teaspoon celery salt
- 1/8 teaspoon garlic powder
- 1 teaspoon extra-virgin olive oil

- 1 tablespoon kosher salt
- ½ pound chicken breast, skinless, boneless
- ¼ teaspoon lemon pepper
- A large pinch smoked paprika
- A pinch ground cardamom

Directions:

1. To make brine: Add water, 2 teaspoons of sugar, and salt into a bowl and stir until sugar dissolves completely.
2. Add chicken and coat it well with the brine. Chill for an hour.
3. Follow the instructions given in the manual and fill the sous vide water oven. Preheat it to 150°F.
4. Add 1 teaspoon butter, ½ teaspoon sugar, celery salt, and all the spices into a bowl. Mix the butter into the spices with a fork.
5. Discard the brine and dry the chicken by patting with paper towels. Smear the chicken with the spice rub and place in a Ziploc bag or vacuum-seal pouch.
6. Vacuum seal the pouch.
7. Submerge the pouch in water bath and adjust the timer for 1½ hours or until cooked through.
8. Remove the pouch from the water bath. Remove the chicken and place on your cutting board. Discard the liquid from the pouch.
9. To finish: Place a skillet over medium heat and add oil and remaining butter. When butter melts, add chicken and cook until golden brown. Flip sides and cook until golden brown.
10. Remove from the pan and let it sit for 5 minutes. Slice and serve.

Chicken Parmigiana

Serves: 8

Ingredients:

For chicken:

- 8 chicken breasts
- 8 sprigs fresh rosemary
- 8 sprigs fresh thyme
- Salt to taste
- Pepper to taste
- 1 teaspoon garlic powder

For breading:

- 1 ½ cups flour
- 2 teaspoons pepper, or to taste
- 1 ½ cups dried Italian bread crumbs
- ¼ cup chopped parsley
- 4 teaspoons salt
- 4 eggs
- ½ cup grated parmesan cheese
- Oil, as required

To finish:

- 1 cup chopped basil
- ½ cup grated parmesan cheese
- 2 cups shredded mozzarella cheese

Directions:

1. Follow the instructions given in the manual and fill the sous vide water oven. Preheat it to 141°F.
2. For chicken: Sprinkle salt, pepper, and garlic powder over the chicken. Place the chicken in 2 or 3 vacuum-seal pouches or Ziploc bags. Divide the herbs among the pouches. Vacuum seal the pouches.
3. Submerge the pouches in the water bath. Set the timer for 2 or 3 hours, or until cooked. Do not stack the pouches.
4. When the timer goes off, remove the pouches from the water bath. Remove the chicken from the pouches and place on a plate. When cool enough to handle, pat the chicken dry with paper towels.
5. Place flour, pepper, and salt on a large plate and mix well.
6. Add eggs into a wide bowl and whisk well.
7. Place breadcrumbs, parsley, and Parmesan cheese on a large plate and mix well.

8. Place a pan over medium heat. Pour enough oil to cover the bottom of the pan by ½ inch and let the oil heat.
9. First, coat the chicken in flour. Next, dip in the beaten egg. Shake to remove excess egg. Finally, dredge in breadcrumbs and place on a plate.
10. When the oil is well heated, add a few pieces of chicken into the pan and cook until golden brown all over.
11. Remove and place on a plate. Cook the remaining pieces in batches.

Turkey Breast with Gravy

Serves: 3 or 4

Ingredients:

For turkey:

- Freshly ground pepper to taste
- Salt to taste
- 1 turkey breast half (about 2.5 to 3 pounds)

For gravy:

- 2 tablespoons vegetable oil
- 2 large carrots, peeled, chopped
- 3 quarts chicken stock
- 2 teaspoons soy sauce
- ½ cup flour
- 2 large onions, chopped
- 4 ribs celery, chopped
- 4 bay leaves
- 6 tablespoons butter

Directions:

1. Follow the instructions given in the manual and fill the sous vide water oven. Preheat it to 132°F to 158°F, depending on how you like your turkey cooked.
2. Cook at 132°F for very pink, soft and extra moist; at 138°F for pale pink, soft and moist; 145°F for white, tender and moist; or at 152°F for white.
3. Gently take out the turkey skin in one piece and set it aside.
4. Take out the breast meat from the breastbone and keep the breastbone.
5. Sprinkle salt and pepper liberally over the turkey.
6. Place the turkey in a large Ziploc bag or vacuum-seal pouch.
7. Vacuum seal the pouch.
8. Submerge the pouch in the water bath and set the timer for 2½ hours or until cooked.
9. Meanwhile, make the gravy and crispy skin as follows: Place a rack in the center in an oven. Preheat the oven to 400°F.
10. Place a sheet of parchment paper on a rimmed baking sheet. Place the skin on the baking sheet. Sprinkle salt and pepper liberally over the turkey skin. Keep another sheet of parchment paper on top of the skin and press lightly.
11. Now place another rimmed baking sheet on top of the parchment paper.
12. Transfer the entire set up of baking sheets to the oven. Roast until skin is brown. Remove the baking sheets from the oven and let it cool. It will be crisp once cooled completely. Break into pieces
13. To make gravy: Cut the breastbone into 1-inch pieces.

14. Place a saucepan over high heat and add oil. When the oil is well heated, add breastbone, carrots, onion, and celery and mix well. Cook until brown.
15. Stir in the bay leaves, stock, and soy sauce. When it begins to boil, lower heat and cook for about 45 minutes, stirring occasionally.
16. Place a wire mesh strainer over a bowl. This is the stock. Pour the mixture into the strainer and throw away the solids.
17. Place a saucepan over medium flame and add butter. When butter melts, stir in the flour and stir constantly until light brown.
18. Drizzle in the broth, stirring constantly. Keep stirring until it comes to a boil.
19. Reduce the heat and simmer until thick. Add salt and pepper to taste.
20. Remove the pouch from the water bath and let it cool for a few minutes.
21. Remove the turkey from the pouch and place on your cutting board. When cool enough to handle, cut into ½-inch thick slices.
22. To serve: Divide the turkey slices onto individual serving plates. Spoon the gravy over the turkey slices.
23. Place crispy turkey skin on top and serve.

Mediterranean Turkey Burgers

Serves: 3

Ingredients:

For burger:

- 1 pound ground turkey
- ½ small onion, grated
- 2 tablespoons chopped basil
- 2 tablespoons chopped parsley
- ½ tablespoons Worcestershire sauce
- ½ teaspoon dry mustard powder
- Salt to taste
- Freshly ground pepper to taste
- ¼ cup sun-dried tomatoes, packed in oil, drained, chopped
- 2 cloves garlic, minced
- Zest of ½ lemon, grated

To serve:

- 3 slices cheese
- 3 tomato slices
- 3 hamburger buns, split
- 3 lettuce leaves
- Any other toppings, condiments, etc. of your choice

Directions:

1. Follow the instructions given in the manual and fill the sous vide water oven. Preheat it to 145°F.
2. Place a sheet of plastic wrap on a small baking sheet.
3. Add all the ingredients for burger into a bowl and mix well.
4. Divide the mixture into 3 equal portions and shape into burgers. Place the burgers on the prepared baking sheet. Place another sheet of plastic wrap over the burgers.
5. Freeze until firm.
6. Place the patties into 3 separate vacuum-seal pouches or Ziploc bags.
7. Vacuum seal the pouch.
8. Submerge the pouch in the water bath and set the timer for 60 minutes.
9. Just before the timer goes off, make an ice water bath by filling a large bowl with water and ice.
10. When done, remove the pouch from the water bath and immerse in the ice water bath. When cooled, remove the pouch from the water bath.
11. Remove the burgers from the pouch and dry them by patting with paper towels.
12. Place a cast iron skillet over medium heat and spray some cooking spray in the pan. Place

the patties in the pan and cook for a minute. Flip sides and cook the other side for a minute.
13. Toast the buns lightly if desired. Place lettuce leaves on the bottom half of the buns. Place a burger on each. Place a tomato slice and a cheese slice on each burger. Top with any other toppings if desired. Cover with the top half of the buns and serve.

Sous Vide Turkey Roulade

Serves: 3

Ingredients:

- 1 turkey breast half
- ½ tablespoon lemon zest, grated
- ½ tablespoon orange zest, grated
- ½ tablespoon kosher salt
- ½ tablespoon fresh parsley, minced
- ½ teaspoon fresh rosemary, minced
- ½ teaspoon fresh thyme minced
- ½ teaspoon garlic, minced
- ½ teaspoon freshly ground black pepper

Directions:

1. Follow the instructions given in the manual and fill the sous vide water oven. Preheat it to 145°F.
2. Mix together all the spices, herbs, and salt in a bowl. Sprinkle this mixture over the inner side of the turkey breast half. Roll the turkey and tie with strings to hold it in place.
3. Place turkey in a large Ziploc bag or vacuum-seal pouch. Vacuum seal the pouch.
4. Submerge the pouch in the water bath and set the timer for 3 hours or until cooked.
5. Remove the pouch from the water bath and let it cool for a few minutes.
6. Remove turkey from the pouch and when it cools down, cut into ½-inch thick slices and serve.

Sous Vide Steak

Serves: 6 to 8

Ingredients:

- 2 steaks (1 inch thick)
- 4 fresh thyme sprigs
- Kosher salt to taste
- Freshly ground pepper to taste

For finishing:

- 2 tablespoons butter
- 2 tablespoons canola oil

Directions:

1. Follow the instructions given in the manual and fill the sous vide water oven. Preheat it to 130°F.
2. Sprinkle salt and pepper generously over the steak.
3. Take 2 vacuum-seal pouches or Ziploc bag. Place a steak in each, then place thyme sprigs on either side of the steak. Vacuum seal the pouches.
4. Submerge the pouches in the water bath and fix on the edge of the water bath with clips.
5. Set the timer for 2 to 3 hours or until cooked.
6. Remove the pouches from the water bath and let it cool for 15 minutes.
7. Remove the steaks from the pouch and place on your cutting board. Dry with paper towels.
8. To finish: Place a cast iron skillet over high heat and allow it to heat. When it just begins to smoke, add oil and swirl the pan so that the oil spreads.
9. Add steak and butter and cook for about 45 seconds. Flip sides and cook for another 45 seconds. Baste with butter as it sears.
10. Remove steak and when it is cool enough to handle, cut into ½-inch thick slices and serve.

Greek Burger with Feta Cream

Serves: 4

Ingredients:

For patties:

- 2.2 pounds 80/20 ground beef
- 2 tablespoons dried oregano
- 2 tablespoons salt
- 2 tablespoons dried marjoram
- 2 tablespoons dried parsley flakes
- 1 tablespoon pepper

For feta cream:

- 1 1/3 cups heavy cream
- 1 tablespoon garlic powder
- 1 teaspoon salt
- 1 cup feta cheese, crumbled
- 2 teaspoons pepper or to taste

To serve:

- 4 burger buns, split
- A handful fresh parsley, chopped
- 1 large red onions, cut into thin round slices
- 4 large lettuce leaves

Directions:

1. Follow the instructions given in the manual and fill the sous vide water oven. Preheat it to 140°F.
2. Add all the ingredients for patties into a bowl and mix well.
3. Divide the mixture into 4 portions and shape into patties.
4. Place the patties into 4 vacuum-seal pouches or Ziploc bags.
5. Vacuum seal the pouch.
6. Submerge the pouch in the water bath and set the timer for 40 minutes.
7. Just before the timer goes off, make an ice water bath by filling a large bowl with water and ice.
8. When done, remove the pouch from the water bath and immerse in the ice water bath. When cooled, remove the pouch from the water bath.
9. Place a cast iron skillet over medium heat. Place the patties in the pan and cook for a minute. Flip sides and cook the other side for a minute.
10. To make feta cream: Add cream and egg yolks into a saucepan. Heat the saucepan over low flame and stir frequently until slightly thick.

11. Add the remaining ingredients and mix well.
12. Toast the buns lightly if desired. Place lettuce leaves on the bottom half of the buns. Place a burger on each. Place onion slices and parsley. Cover with the top bun and serve.

Short Rib Tacos

Serves: 2

Ingredients:

- 1 pound thinly cut short ribs (2 pieces)
- 2 green onions, sliced
- 3 cloves garlic, peeled, chopped
- ½ inch ginger, peeled, grated
- ¼ teaspoon red pepper powder
- ¼ cup soy sauce
- ½ tablespoon sambal oelek or chili paste
- 1 tablespoon brown sugar
- ½ tablespoon sesame oil

<u>To finish:</u>

- Kimchi
- 4 corn tortillas
- Few avocado slices

Directions:

1. Follow the instructions given in the manual and fill the sous vide water oven. Preheat it to 138°F.
2. Place short ribs in a large vacuum-seal pouch or Ziploc bag.
3. Add remaining ingredients in a saucepan and place the saucepan over medium heat. Stir frequently until sugar dissolves completely. Turn off the heat and let it cool completely.
4. Pour into the pouch over the short ribs. Vacuum seal the pouch.
5. Submerge the pouch in the water bath and set the timer for 2 hours.
6. To finish: Set the oven to broiler mode and preheat.
7. Remove the pouch from the water bath and pour the liquid from the pouch into a saucepan. Place the saucepan over medium flame and simmer until thick. Turn off the heat.
8. Remove the short ribs and place on a baking sheet.
9. Place in the oven and broil for a few minutes, until crisp.
10. Remove the short ribs and cut into small cubes.
11. To assemble: Place tortillas on a large serving platter. Place short ribs on the tortillas. Garnish with kimchi and avocado slices. Drizzle the thickened sauce on top and serve.

Pot Roast

Serves: 2 or 3

Ingredients:

- 1 pound chuck roast
- 2 tablespoons soy sauce
- 2 small sprigs fresh rosemary
- 2 tablespoons lemon juice
- ½ teaspoon minced garlic

<u>To finish:</u>

- 1 tablespoon olive oil

Directions:

1. Follow the instructions given in the manual and fill the sous vide water oven. Preheat it to 130° to 140°F, depending on how you like your roast cooked. Cook at 130° for medium-rare or at 140° for medium-well.
2. Add all the ingredients except meat into a bowl and stir. Pour into a vacuum-seal pouch or Ziploc bag. Place the meat in the pouch.
3. Vacuum seal the pouch.
4. Submerge the pouch in the water bath and set the timer for 18 to 24 hours. Remove the pouch from the water bath after about 9 to 10 hours of cooking. Shake the bag a few times and place it back in the water bath.
5. When the timer goes off, remove the pouch from the water bath.
6. Place a saucepan over medium heat and add oil. When the oil is heated, add roast and cook for a minute. Flip sides and cook the other side for a minute.
7. Remove from the pan. When it cools down, cut into slices.
8. Serve.

Pork Belly Adobo

Serves: 4

Ingredients:

- 1.1 pounds pork belly, cut into cubes
- 2 tablespoons soy sauce
- ½ tablespoon sugar
- 4 cloves garlic, crushed
- 2-3 pieces chili
- 2 tablespoons coconut vinegar
- ½ cup coconut cream
- ½ tablespoon black peppercorns
- ½ tablespoon olive oil
- 2 bay leaves
- Salt to taste

Directions:

1. Follow the instructions given in the manual and fill the sous vide water oven. Preheat it to 158°F.
2. Sprinkle salt over the pork.
3. Place a skillet over medium heat and add oil. When the oil is heated, add pork and cook until browned all over. Remove pork with a slotted spoon and set aside on a plate.
4. Add garlic and peppercorns to the skillet and sauté for a few seconds until garlic is fragrant.
5. Add rest of the ingredients and stir. Lower the heat and simmer until sauce reduces to ¼. Turn off the heat.
6. Place pork in a Ziploc bag or vacuum-seal pouch. Spoon the sauce over the pork. Turn the pouch around to coat evenly. Vacuum seal the pouch.
7. Submerge the pouch into the water bath and set the timer for 18 to 24 hours, depending on how you like your pork cooked.
8. Remove the pouch from the water bath and cool for a few minutes. Remove pork from the pouch and serve.

Perfect Double-Cut Rosemary Infused Pork Chop with Hard Cider Caramel Sauce

Serves: 2

Ingredients:

- 2 bone-in, double cut pork chops (1 pound each)
- 2 sprigs rosemary, chopped
- 2 cups hard cider, divided
- 2 tablespoons dark brown sugar
- Kosher salt to taste
- Freshly ground pepper to taste
- 2 cloves garlic, peeled, chopped
- 2 tablespoons vegetable oil

To serve:

- Sautéed apples
- Sautéed cabbage

Directions:

1. Follow the instructions given in the manual and fill the sous vide water oven. Preheat it to 140°F.
2. Sprinkle salt and pepper liberally over the pork chops.
3. Sprinkle rosemary and garlic. Rub it into the chops and place in a large Ziploc bag or vacuum-seal pouch. Pour a cup of hard cider into the pouch.
4. Vacuum seal the pouch.
5. Submerge the pouch into the water bath and set the timer for 2 hours.
6. When done, remove the steaks from the pouch and place on your cutting board. Dry with paper towels.
7. To finish: Place a cast iron skillet over high heat and allow it to heat. When it just begins to smoke, add oil and swirl the pan so that the oil spreads.
8. Place pork chops in the skillet and cook for about 45 seconds. Flip and cook the other side for 45 seconds.
9. Remove pork with a slotted spoon and place on individual serving plates.
10. Pour the cooked liquids from the pouch into the skillet. Add remaining hard cider and sugar, and stir until sugar dissolves completely and the sauce is well heated. Turn off the heat.
11. Spoon the sauce over the pork chops and serve with the suggested serving options.

Lamb Chops with Orange

Serves: 4

Ingredients:

- 4 lamb rib chops
- ¼ cup orange juice
- 1 teaspoon orange zest, grated
- 1 tablespoon vegetable oil
- Salt to taste
- ¼ teaspoon dried thyme
- 1 tablespoon honey

To finish:

- 1 tablespoon cornstarch mixed with 1 tablespoon water

Directions:

1. Follow the instructions given in the manual and fill the sous vide water oven. Preheat it to 132°F.
2. Add orange juice, orange zest, oil, salt, thyme, and honey into a bowl and stir. Transfer into a Ziploc bag or vacuum-seal pouch.
3. Add lamb chops.
4. Arrange the lamb chops in a single layer. Vacuum seal the pouch.
5. Submerge the pouch in water bath and adjust the timer for 2 hours.
6. When the timer goes off, remove the pouch from the water bath.
7. To make sauce: Add the cooked liquid from the pouch into a skillet over medium flame. Add cornstarch mixture. Stir constantly until thick.
8. Spoon the sauce over the lamb chops and serve.

Leg of Lamb with Rosemary and Garlic

Serves: 4

Ingredients:

- 2 large cloves garlic, peeled, minced
- 2 boneless leg of lamb (1 pound each)
- 2 teaspoons extra-virgin olive oil
- 2 tablespoons chopped onions
- 4 tablespoons dry red wine
- 2 tablespoons chopped fresh rosemary
- Salt to taste
- Freshly ground pepper to taste
- 2 tablespoons unsalted butter
- 2 tablespoons all-purpose flour
- 1 ½ cups beef stock

Directions:

1. Follow the instructions given in the manual and fill the sous vide water oven. Preheat it to 131°F.
2. Add garlic and rosemary in a bowl and rub mixture all over the lamb. Sprinkle with salt and pepper, then drizzle with oil and rub it in well.
3. Place leg of lamb in 2 pouches. Vacuum seal the pouches.
4. Set the timer for 8 hours. Use plastic wrap to cover the water bath. This helps to reduce water evaporation.
5. Just before the timer goes off, set an oven to broiler mode and preheat.
6. Remove the pouch from the water bath. Take out only the lamb from the pouch and dry the lamb by patting with paper towels.
7. Broil the lamb for about 5 minutes or until brown on top.
8. Meanwhile, place a skillet over medium heat and add butter. When butter melts, add onion and sauté for a minute.
9. Add flour and whisk well. Pour the cooked liquid from the pouch and wine and stir constantly until smooth.
10. Add stock and whisk well. When the sauce begins to bubble, reduce the heat and cook until thick. Stir frequently. Add salt and pepper to taste.
11. Remove lamb from the oven and place on your cutting board. When cool enough to handle, cut into slices.
12. Spoon the sauce over the lamb slices and serve.

Lamb Chops with Chimichurri Compound Butter

Serves: 4

Ingredients:

- 8 lamb chops or shoulder chops
- Salt to taste
- Pepper to taste
- ¼ cup chopped fresh oregano
- 2 tablespoons champagne vinegar
- ½ teaspoon crushed red pepper flakes
- 2/3 cup salted butter, softened
- Avocado oil, as required
- 2 cups firmly packed, minced fresh parsley
- 2 cloves garlic, finely minced
- 2 tablespoons fresh lime juice

Directions:

1. Follow the instructions given in the manual and fill the sous vide water oven. Preheat it to 132°F.
2. Sprinkle salt and pepper generously over the lamb and place in 2 large Ziploc bags or vacuum-seal pouches. Vacuum seal the pouches.
3. Submerge the pouches into the water bath and set the timer for 2 hours.
4. To make chimichurri compound butter: Add rest of the ingredients into a bowl. Mix well. Cover and refrigerate until use.
5. When the timer goes off, remove the pouches from the water bath. Remove the lamb from the pouches and dry the lamb by patting with paper towels. Sprinkle with salt and pepper.
6. Place a large cast iron skillet over high heat and add oil. Swirl the pan so that the oil spreads. When oil heats, add the lamb chops and cook on both sides for a minute until golden brown. Cook in batches.
7. Serve with a big spoonful of chimichurri compound butter.

Tilapia with Tomato, Olives and Oregano

Serves: 4

Ingredients:

- 2 pounds skinless tilapia fillets
- Juice of 2 lemons
- 2 cloves, minced
- ½ teaspoon celery seeds
- 4 tablespoons dried breadcrumbs
- 4 tablespoons tomato paste
- 4 tablespoons extra-virgin olive oil

To serve:

- Few lemon slices
- A handful fresh parsley, chopped
- 4 black olives, pitted, chopped
- 2 teaspoons dried oregano
- Salt to taste
- Freshly ground pepper to taste

Directions:

1. Follow the instructions given in the manual and fill the sous vide water oven. Preheat it to 134°F.
2. Dry the fillets by patting with paper towels and place in a large Ziploc bag or vacuum-seal pouch.
3. Add lemon juice, 2 tablespoons oil, oregano, salt, garlic, pepper, and celery seeds into a bowl and mix well. Pour into the pouch, over the fish. Turn the fish around in the pouch so that it is well coated with the mixture.
4. Vacuum seal the pouch.
5. Submerge the pouch in water bath and adjust the timer for 30 minutes.
6. Just before the timer goes off, set an oven to broiler mode and preheat.
7. Remove the pouch from the water bath. Take out the fillets from the pouch.
8. Add breadcrumbs and remaining oil into a bowl and mix well. Dredge the fillets in the breadcrumbs and place in a baking dish.
9. Broil the fillets for about 2 to 3 minutes or until brown on top.
10. Top with the suggested serving options and serve.

Creamy Thai Red Curry with Fish

Serves: 4

Ingredients:

- 4 barramundi or sea bass fillets
- 4 tablespoons vegetable oil
- 4 tablespoons red curry paste
- 2 cups chopped eggplants (chopped into chunks)
- 4 pieces (2 inches each) lemon grass, bruised
- 2 cups chicken stock
- 4 tablespoons lemon juice
- 2 ¼ cups coconut milk
- ¼ cup chopped fresh cilantro,
- 2 red onion, chopped into chunks
- 4 cloves garlic, peeled, diced
- 2 tablespoons palm sugar
- Salt to taste
- Hot cooked rice to serve

Directions:

1. Follow the instructions given in the manual and fill the sous vide water oven. Preheat it to 135°F.
2. Place fish fillets in a large vacuum-seal pouch or Ziploc bag. Pour ¼ cup coconut milk into it.
3. Vacuum seal the pouch.
4. Submerge the pouch in the water bath and adjust the timer for 30 minutes.
5. In the meantime, place a skillet over medium heat and add oil. When the oil is heated, add onions, garlic, and eggplant and sauté for a few minutes. Add red curry paste and stir until aromatic. Mix in the lemongrass, remaining coconut milk, and stock.
6. Reduce the heat and simmer for 15 to 20 minutes. Add lime juice, palm sugar, and salt and stir until sugar is dissolved. Remove from heat.
7. Add fish and stir, then serve over rice.

Sous Vide Lemon Cod

Serves: 4

Ingredients:

- 4 cod fillets (6 ounces each)
- 2 tablespoons extra-virgin olive oil
- Kosher salt to taste
- Freshly ground pepper to taste
- Zest of 2 lemons, grated
- Juice of 2 lemons, grated

Directions:

1. Follow the instructions given in the manual and fill the sous vide water oven. Preheat it to 135°F.
2. Sprinkle salt and pepper over the fillets and place in 1 or 2 large vacuum-seal pouches or Ziploc bags.
3. Add remaining ingredients into the pouch and vacuum seal.
4. Submerge the pouch in the water bath and adjust the timer for 30 minutes.
5. When the cook time is over, remove the pouches from the water bath. Remove the fillets from the pouches and dry them by patting with paper towels, then serve.

Eggplant Lasagna

Serves: 8

Ingredients:

- 4 pounds eggplants, peeled, cut into thin rounds
- 3 cups tomato sauce (for recipe, refer to chapter on sauces)
- 4 ounces parmesan cheese, grated
- ½ cup chopped fresh basil
- 4 teaspoons kosher salt
- 8 ounces fresh mozzarella cheese, thinly sliced
- 8 ounces Italian blend cheese, grated
- 2 tablespoons seasoned breadcrumbs

Directions:

1. Follow the instructions given in the manual and fill the sous vide water oven. Preheat it to 189°F.
2. Place a colander in the sink. Place eggplants in the colander and sprinkle salt on both sides of the eggplant slices. Let them sit in the colander for 30 minutes.
3. Rinse well and dry them by patting with paper towels.
4. Place a large Ziploc bag or vacuum-seal pouches flat on its side on your countertop. Let it hang open.
5. Place half the eggplant slices inside the bag on the flat side, slightly overlapping.
6. Spread 1 cup tomato sauce over the eggplant slices. Layer with mozzarella cheese followed by 2 ounces Parmesan cheese. Sprinkle 6 ounces Italian cheese blend.
7. Sprinkle basil. Place remaining eggplant slices, slightly overlapping. Spread 1 cup tomato sauce over it.
8. Vacuum seal the bag, keeping it flat.
9. Submerge the pouch by placing it flat in the water bath and let it remain for 3 hours. You may need to remove air during the initial 30 minutes of cooking, as the eggplants will release some gasses.
10. When done, lift the pouch flat from the water bath and place on a plate. Snip one of the corners of the pouch and gently tilt to remove excess liquid.
11. Now place the bag flat on an ovenproof plate or rimmed baking dish. Cut the pouch and carefully slide the lasagna onto the plate. Let it rest for 10 minutes. Remove any excess liquid.
12. Spread remaining tomato sauce over it. Sprinkle breadcrumbs and remaining cheeses.
13. Broil for a few minutes until the cheese is brown.
14. You can serve it over pasta along with a side dish, or use it as a filling for sandwiches.

Chili-Garlic Tofu

Serves: 8

Ingredients:

- 2 blocks firm tofu, cut into slices
- 1 cup brown sugar
- 4 tablespoons chili-garlic paste
- ½ cup soy sauce
- ½ cup sesame oil

Directions:

1. Follow the instructions given in the manual and fill the sous vide water oven. Preheat it to 180°F.
2. Place a skillet over medium heat and add 2 or 3 tablespoons oil. Add half the tofu and cook well. Remove and place on paper towels.
3. Cook the remaining tofu similarly. Turn off the heat.
4. Add remaining ingredients into a bowl and mix well. Add tofu and mix well. Transfer into a large Ziploc bag or vacuum-seal pouch.
5. Vacuum seal the pouch.
6. Submerge the pouch in the water bath and adjust the timer for 4 hours.
7. Remove from the pouch and add into a bowl. Mix well and serve.

Rotini in Saffron-Tomato Oil

Serves: 8

Ingredients:

- 2.2 pounds ripe tomatoes, cut into wedges
- A large pinch saffron threads
- Red pepper flakes to taste
- Salt to taste
- 2 cups olive oil
- 2 heads garlic, finely chopped
- 2 tablespoons black peppercorns, cracked
- 1.1 pounds rotini

To serve:

- A handful fresh parsley, chopped
- 2 cups grated parmesan cheese

Directions:

1. Follow the instructions given in the manual and fill the sous vide water oven. Preheat it to 185°F.
2. Add all the ingredients except pasta into a large Ziploc bag or vacuum-seal pouch.
3. Vacuum seal the pouch.
4. Submerge the pouch in the water bath and adjust the timer for 1 hour.
5. Meanwhile, cook the pasta following the directions on the package.
6. Place pasta in a large bowl.
7. Remove the pouch from the water bath and pour the tomato mixture over the pasta. Toss well.
8. Divide into 8 serving bowls. Top with Parmesan and parsley and serve.

Hearty Rice Bowl

Serves: 2

Ingredients:

- 2/3 cup rice
- 2/3 cup + 2 tablespoons water
- Salt to taste
- 2 teaspoons fresh lime juice
- 1 teaspoon cumin seeds
- 8 ounces shiitake mushrooms, sliced
- 2 teaspoons tamari or soy sauce
- 4 teaspoons unsalted butter, divided
- 2 large carrots, peeled, cut into ½-inch pieces
- 2 teaspoons pure maple syrup
- 2 ½ teaspoons toasted sesame oil, divided
- ½ teaspoon cornstarch

To serve:

- Sous vide poached eggs
- A dash of hot sauce
- 2 scallions, sliced
- Roasted, crushed peanuts
- Any other toppings of your choice

Directions:

1. Follow the instructions given in the manual and fill the sous vide water oven. Preheat it to 190°F.
2. Add rice, 1 teaspoon salt, 2 teaspoons butter and water into a large Ziploc bag or vacuum-seal pouch.
3. Shake the pouch so that the ingredients are well combined.
4. Add carrots, maple syrup, 2 teaspoons butter, lime juice, cumin, a little salt and ½ teaspoon oil into another large vacuum pouch. Shake the pouch so that the ingredients are well combined.
5. Add mushrooms, tamari, cornstarch, 2 teaspoons oil and a little salt into one more vacuum pouch. Shake the pouch so that the ingredients are well combined.
6. Vacuum seal the pouches.
7. Submerge the pouches in the water bath and adjust the timer for 1 hour or until the vegetables and rice are cooked.
8. Remove the pouches from the water bath. Divide the rice into 2 bowls.
9. Divide the mushrooms among the bowls. Remove the carrots from the pouch and place over the mushrooms.
10. Top with the suggested toppings. Pour the liquid from the carrot pouch on top and serve.

CHAPTER THIRTEEN
SOUS VIDE SIDE DISH RECIPES

Butter-Poached Potatoes

Serves: 4

Ingredients:

- 2 pounds small Yukon gold potatoes, halved
- 2 tablespoons extra-virgin olive oil
- Salt to taste
- 4 tablespoons unsalted butter
- 2 tablespoons minced fresh thyme or rosemary (optional)
- Freshly ground pepper to taste

Directions:

1. Follow the instructions given in the manual and fill the sous vide water oven. Preheat it to 190°F.
2. Add all the ingredients into a large Ziploc bag or vacuum-seal pouch.
3. Vacuum seal the pouch.
4. Submerge the pouch in the water bath and adjust the timer for 1 hour. When cook time is over, remove the pouch from the water bath. Empty the contents of the pouch in a bowl.
5. Mix well and serve.

Garlic Cheese Risotto

Serves: 8

Ingredients:

- 2 cups Arborio rice
- 6 cups vegetable broth
- Salt to taste
- Pepper to taste
- 2 teaspoons extra-virgin olive oil
- 4 tablespoons jarred roasted garlic, minced
- 2 sprigs fresh rosemary leaves, minced
- 2/3 cup grated Romano cheese

Directions:

1. Follow the instructions given in the manual and fill the sous vide water oven. Preheat it to 183°F.
2. Add all the ingredients except cheese into a large Ziploc bag or vacuum-seal pouch.
3. Vacuum seal the pouch.
4. Submerge the pouch in water bath and set the timer for 45 minutes or until rice is cooked.
5. Remove the pouch from the water bath. Empty the contents into a warm serving bowl. Fluff the rice with a fork. Add cheese and mix well.
6. Serve hot.

Sous Vide Glazed Carrots Recipe

Serves: 8 to 10

Ingredients:

- 2 pounds whole baby carrots, scrubbed
- 2 tablespoons granulated sugar
- Freshly ground pepper to taste
- 4 tablespoons unsalted butter
- Kosher salt to taste
- 2 tablespoons chopped parsley (optional)

Directions:

1. Follow the instructions given in the manual and fill the sous vide water oven. Preheat it to 183°F.
2. Add carrots, sugar, butter, and about a teaspoon of salt in a vacuum-seal pouch or Ziploc bag.
3. Vacuum seal the pouch.
4. Submerge the pouch in water bath and set the timer for 45 to 60 minutes, or until tender.
5. Remove the pouch from the water bath and refrigerate until use.
6. To serve: Add all the contents of the pouch into a heavy bottomed skillet and place the skillet over high heat.
7. Stir frequently until the carrots are glossy and coated with the liquid in the pan.
8. Add salt, pepper, and parsley and mix well.
9. Serve hot.

Sous Vide Mashed Potatoes

Serves: 2 or 3

Ingredients:

- 1 pound russet potato, peeled, cut into ⅛-inch thick slices
- 2 sprigs rosemary
- ½ cup whole milk
- 3 cloves garlic, peeled, smashed
- 4 ounces unsalted butter
- 1 teaspoon kosher salt, or to taste

Directions:

1. Follow the instructions given in the manual and fill the sous vide water oven. Preheat it to 194°F.
2. Add all the ingredients into a large Ziploc bag or vacuum-seal pouch.
3. Vacuum seal the pouch.
4. Submerge the pouch in the water bath and adjust the timer for 1 ½ hours.
5. When cook time is over, remove the pouch from the water bath.
6. Empty the contents of the pouch into a wire mesh strainer placed over a bowl. Retain the cooked liquid. Remove and discard the rosemary.
7. Add potatoes into another bowl and mash with a potato masher until smooth. Add as much cooked liquid as required into the bowl of potatoes and mix well.
8. Serve.

Sous Vide Brussels Sprouts

Serves: 8

Ingredients:

- 2 pounds Brussels sprouts, trimmed
- 4 cloves garlic, peeled, smashed, minced
- Freshly ground pepper to taste
- Salt to taste
- 2 tablespoons olive oil

To finish:

- Bamboo skewers

Directions:

1. Follow the instructions given in the manual and fill the sous vide water oven. Preheat it to 180°F.
2. Add all the ingredients into a bowl and mix well. Transfer into a Ziploc bag or vacuum-seal pouch.
3. Vacuum seal the pouch.
4. Submerge the pouch in the water bath and adjust the timer for 1 hour.
5. When cook time is over, remove the pouch from the water bath.
6. To finish: Soak the bamboo skewers for 20 minutes. Thread the Brussels sprouts onto the skewers.
7. Preheat a grill. Place the skewers on the grill and grill for 2 to 3 minutes.

Roasted Okra with Curried Lemon Yogurt

Serves: 4

Ingredients:

- 1 pound fresh okra, rinsed, dried with kitchen towel, trimmed
- 1 ½ tablespoons extra-virgin olive oil
- ½ tablespoon red curry paste
- 2 tablespoons chopped fresh mint
- Salt to taste
- ½ tablespoon + ½ teaspoon grated lemon zest
- ½ cup fresh Greek yogurt
- 2 tablespoons chopped fresh cilantro

Directions:

1. Follow the instructions given in the manual and fill the sous vide water oven. Preheat it to 180°F.
2. Place okra in a large bowl and season with salt. Sprinkle ½ teaspoon lemon zest and drizzle ½ tablespoon oil. Toss well.
3. Transfer into a large vacuum-seal pouch or Ziploc bag. Spread it evenly in a single layer. Vacuum seal the pouch.
4. Submerge the pouch in the water bath and adjust the timer for 1 hour.
5. When cook time is over, remove the pouch from the water bath. Drain the cooked liquid into a bowl. Add curry paste, yogurt, and ½ tablespoon zest and mix well. Cover and set aside for a while.
6. Meanwhile, dry the okra by patting with paper towels.
7. Place a skillet over medium-high flame and add a tablespoon of oil. When the oil is heated, add okra and cook for a few minutes until golden brown and crisp.
8. Add salt, mint, and cilantro and toss well.
9. Serve with yogurt sauce. You can spoon the sauce over the okra or serve it separately.

Swedish Potato Casserole

Serves: 2 or 3

Ingredients:

- 1 pound potatoes, peeled, shredded
- Salt to taste
- White pepper to taste
- 1.75 ounces Swedish sprats in oil or rinsed anchovies, chopped
- ¼ cup dry breadcrumbs
- 1 onion, thinly sliced
- 2 tablespoons unsalted butter, chopped into small cubes + extra to grease
- 1 cup heavy cream

Directions:

1. Follow the instructions given in the manual and fill the sous vide water oven. Preheat it to 185°F.
2. Place potatoes in a bowl. Sprinkle with salt and pepper and toss well.
3. Transfer into a vacuum-seal pouch or Ziploc bag. Spread evenly in a single layer. Vacuum seal the pouch.
4. Place onions in the bowl. Sprinkle with salt and pepper and toss well.
5. Transfer into another vacuum-seal pouch or Ziploc bag. Spread evenly in a single layer. Vacuum seal the pouch.
6. Submerge the pouches in the water bath and adjust the timer for 45 to 60 minutes.
7. Just before the timer goes off, make an ice water bath by filling a large bowl with water and ice.
8. When done, remove the pouch from the water bath and immerse in the ice water bath. When cooled, remove the pouch from the water bath.
9. Meanwhile, grease a small casserole dish with some melted butter.
10. Spread 1/3 of the potatoes on the bottom of the dish.
11. Layer with half the onions followed by half the sprats.
12. Place 1/3 of the butter cubes at different places all over the sprats.
13. Repeat steps 10 through 12. Spread remaining potatoes on top.
14. Top with breadcrumbs. Place remaining butter cubes on top.
15. Place casserole dish on a baking sheet.
16. Bake in a preheated oven at 350°F until brown on top.

Arroz Braziliero (Brazilian Rice)

Serves: 3

Ingredients:

- ¾ cup rice
- 1 onion, finely chopped
- 2 tablespoons olive oil
- ¾ cup vegetable stock or chicken stock
- ½ can (from a 14-ounce can) diced tomatoes with its juice
- Pepper to taste
- 1 onion, finely chopped
- Salt to taste
- A handful fresh cilantro, chopped, to garnish

Directions:

1. Follow the instructions given in the manual and fill the sous vide water oven. Preheat it to 183°F.
2. Heat a skillet over medium flame and add oil. When the oil is heated, add onions and sauté until onion turns translucent.
3. Stir in the rice. Stir fry for a couple of minutes until the rice becomes opaque.
4. Turn off the heat and let it cool for a few minutes.
5. Add stock, salt, pepper, and tomatoes and mix well.
6. Transfer the rice into a large vacuum-seal pouch or Ziploc bag. Spread evenly in a single layer. Vacuum seal the pouch.
7. Submerge the pouch in the water bath and adjust the timer for 45 minutes.
8. When the timer goes off, remove the pouch from the water bath.
9. Empty the contents of the pouch into a serving bowl. Loosen the rice with a fork.
10. Sprinkle cilantro on top.
11. Serve right away.

CHAPTER FOURTEEN
SOUS VIDE DESSERT RECIPES

Chocolate Bean Pots de Crème

Serves: 10

Ingredients:

- 14 large egg yolks
- 4 bars dark chocolate (12.6 ounces in all) + extra shaved chocolate to serve
- 4 cups heavy whipping cream + extra to serve
- 1 cup granulated sugar
- A large pinch kosher salt

Directions:

1. Follow the instructions given in the manual and fill the sous vide water oven. Preheat it to 180°F.
2. Add chocolate and heavy cream in a saucepan and place over medium heat. Stir frequently until chocolate melts completely. Remove from heat and let cool slightly if it is very hot.
3. Add yolks, sugar, and vanilla into a blender and blend until smooth. Transfer into a bowl.
4. Add a little of the cream mixture into the egg mixture and whisk. Continue adding a little at a time, whisking well each time. Cool for a while.
5. Pour the mixture into 10 canning jars.
6. Fasten the lid lightly, but not very tight.
7. Submerge the canning jars in water bath and adjust the timer for 90 minutes. Cook in batches if necessary.
8. When the timer goes off, remove the jars and cool completely. Chill for 4 to 5 hours and serve.
9. Garnish with heavy cream and chocolate shavings and serve.

Pumpkin Pie

Serves: 12

Ingredients:

- 2 large cans pumpkins
- ¼ cup flour
- 2 tablespoons pumpkin pie spice
- 1 cup brown sugar
- 1 cup white sugar
- 2 eggs
- 6 egg yolks
- 1 teaspoon kosher salt
- 2 cans evaporated milk
- Whipped cream/crushed candied nuts to serve (optional)

Directions:

1. Follow the instructions given in the manual and fill the sous vide water oven. Preheat it to 175°F.
2. Add all the ingredients into a bowl and whisk well.
3. Pour the mixture into 12 canning jars.
4. Fasten the lid lightly, but not very tight.
5. Submerge the canning jars in water bath and adjust the timer for 60 minutes. Cook in batches if required.
6. When the timer goes off, remove the jars and cool completely. Chill for 4 to 5 hours and serve.

Red Wine-Poached Pears

Serves: 8

Ingredients:

- 8 ripe Bosc pears, peeled
- 1 cup granulated sugar
- 2 teaspoons salt
- 2 vanilla beans, scrape the seeds
- 2 cups red wine
- ½ cup sweet vermouth
- 6 pieces (3 inches each) orange zest

To serve:

- Vanilla ice cream

Directions:

1. Follow the instructions given in the manual and fill the sous vide water oven. Preheat it to 175°F.
2. Add all the ingredients into a large Ziploc bag or vacuum-seal pouch.
3. Vacuum seal the pouch.
4. Submerge the pouch in the water bath and adjust the timer for 1 hour.
5. When the timer goes off, remove the bag from the water bath. Take out the pears and place them on your cutting board. Retain the cooked liquid. When pears are cool enough to handle, core the pears and cut into slices.
6. Divide the pear slices into 8 bowls. Scoop vanilla ice cream on top. Spoon some of the cooked liquid on top and serve.

Strawberry Mousse

Serves: 4

Ingredients:

- ½ pound strawberries
- 1 ½ tablespoons fresh lemon juice
- ¼ teaspoon ground cinnamon
- ½ teaspoon vanilla extract
- 2 tablespoons very fine sugar
- ¼ teaspoon kosher salt
- ½ cup heavy cream

Directions:

1. Follow the instructions given in the manual and fill the sous vide water oven. Preheat it to 180°F.
2. Add all the ingredients except vanilla and cream into a vacuum-seal pouch or Ziploc bag.
3. Vacuum seal the pouch.
4. Submerge the pouch in the water bath and adjust the timer for 45 minutes.
5. When done, remove the pouch from the water bath. Empty the contents of the pouch into a blender and blend until smooth. Let it cool completely.
6. Add cream and vanilla into a chilled bowl. Whisk until stiff peaks are formed.
7. Add strawberry puree and fold gently, but do not whisk.
8. Spoon into dessert bowls. Chill for a few hours and serve.

Grasshopper Cheesecake

Serves: 12

Ingredients:

- 4 large chocolate graham crackers, finely crushed
- 2 blocks cream cheese (8 ounces each), softened
- 6 eggs
- 4 drops green food coloring (optional)
- 1 cup chocolate chips
- 4 tablespoons butter, melted
- 1 cup sugar
- 1 teaspoon mint extract
- ½ cup cream
- Andes candy chocolates, to garnish

Directions:

1. Follow the instructions given in the manual and fill the sous vide water oven. Preheat it to 176°F.
2. For crust: Add graham cracker crumbs and butter into a bowl and mix until crumbly.
3. Divide the mixture among 12 jars (4 ounces each). Press it well onto the bottom of the jars.
4. For the cheesecake filling: Add cream cheese and sugar into a large mixing bowl. Beat with an electric hand mixer until light and creamy.
5. Beat in the eggs well.
6. Beat in the mint extract and food coloring if using.
7. Divide the filling among the jars, then fasten the lids of the jar lightly. It should not be tight.
8. Submerge the canning jars in water bath and adjust the timer for 60 minutes. Cook in batches if required.
9. When the timer goes off, remove the jars and cool completely. Chill for 4 to 5 hours and serve.
10. To make ganache: Add cream into a large bowl. Place in the microwave and cook for about a minute or until it is steaming.
11. Remove the bowl from the microwave and add chocolate chips. Whisk until chocolate dissolves completely. Let it cool slightly.
12. Spoon over the cheesecake. Garnish with chocolate on top and serve warm.

Rice and Raisin Pudding

Serves: 3

Ingredients:

- ½ cup basmati rice
- 1 cup skim milk
- ½ tablespoon butter
- 3 teaspoons golden raisins
- 3 teaspoons maple syrup, or to taste
- 1 teaspoon ground cinnamon + extra for serving

Directions:

1. Follow the instructions given in the manual and fill the sous vide water oven. Preheat it to 180°F.
2. Toss all ingredients in a Ziploc bag and vacuum seal the pouch.
3. Submerge the bag into the water bath and cook for 45 to 60 minutes.
4. Remove the pouch from water. Mix well and serve warm or chilled.

Salted Caramel Ice Cream

Serves: 12

Ingredients:

- 3 cups sugar
- 2 teaspoons sea salt
- 10 egg yolks
- A pinch kosher salt
- 3 ½ cups heavy cream
- 2 cups whole milk
- 2 teaspoons vanilla bean paste

Directions:

1. Follow the instructions given in the manual and fill the sous vide water oven. Preheat it to 176°F.
2. Place a non-stick pan over medium heat. Add 2 cups sugar and stir frequently. The sugar will start melting. The color will be pale initially but will turn golden brown.
3. When the sugar turns golden brown, add 2 cups cream and whisk well. Stir constantly until the mixture is well combined. Add sea salt and stir. Turn off the heat. Whisk for a couple of minutes, then cool completely.
4. Add egg yolks, kosher salt, vanilla, milk, and remaining cream and sugar into a blender and blend until smooth.
5. Pour into a large vacuum-seal pouch or Ziploc bag.
6. Vacuum seal the pouch.
7. Submerge the pouch in the water bath and adjust the timer for 30 minutes. Shake the pouch a few times while it is cooking.
8. Remove the pouch from the water bath and add the caramel mixture. Shake until well combined and place in a bowl of ice to chill instantly.
9. Pour into the ice cream maker and churn following the manufacturer's instructions.
10. Serve right away for soft serve ice cream or transfer to a freezer-safe container and freeze until firm.

Crème Brulee, With Different Flavor Options

Serves: 8

Ingredients:

- 4 cups heavy cream
- 8 large egg yolks
- 1 teaspoon vanilla extract
- ½ cup granulated sugar or xylitol + extra to top

Flavor options: (Use any one)

- 8 to 10 saffron threads
- 2 teaspoons rose water
- 2 tablespoons grated lemon or lime or orange zest
- 4 tablespoons instant coffee
- Different flavored extract like almond or peppermint, etc.
- 2 teaspoons orange blossom water
- Any other flavors of your choice

Directions:

1. Follow the instructions given in the manual and fill the sous vide water oven. Preheat it to 195°F.
2. Place a pan over medium-low heat. Add cream and warm it.
3. Add the chosen flavoring and stir. Remove from heat.
4. Meanwhile, add yolks and sugar into a bowl and whisk until the sugar dissolves completely and is light in color.
5. Add a ladle of the warmed cream into the bowl of eggs and whisk well. Repeat until all the cream has been added, a little at a time, and whisk well each time.
6. Divide into 8 Mason jars. Fasten the lids lightly, not very tight.
7. Submerge the jars in water bath and adjust the timer for 40 minutes. Cook in batches if required.
8. When the timer goes off, remove the jars and cool completely.
9. Refrigerate until use.
10. To serve: Sprinkle sugar on top. Use a culinary torch and caramelize the sugar until golden brown.
11. Serve immediately.

Brioche Bread Pudding

Serves: 8

Ingredients:

- 2 cups whole milk
- 1 cup granulated sugar
- 2 large eggs
- 4 large egg yolks
- 2 tablespoons grated orange zest
- 1 teaspoon kosher salt
- 2 cups heavy cream
- ½ cup maple syrup
- 4 tablespoons orange juice
- 2 teaspoons vanilla bean paste or 2 whole vanilla beans, split lengthwise
- 8 cups cubed brioche

Directions:

1. Follow the instructions given in the manual and fill the sous vide water oven. Preheat it to 170°F.
2. Add all the ingredients except brioche into a large bowl and whisk well.
3. Stir in the brioche. Mix until well coated.
4. Take 8 canning jars and divide the mixture among the jars. Fasten the lid lightly, not very tight.
5. Submerge the canning jars in water bath and adjust the timer for 2 hours. Cook in batches, if necessary.
6. When the timer goes off, remove the jars from the water bath and place on a baking sheet.
7. Set an oven to broil mode. Place baking sheet in the oven. Broil for a few minutes until golden brown on top.
8. Remove from the oven and serve.

CONCLUSION

I want to thank you once again for choosing this book.

Now that you have gone through all the information and recipes provided in these pages, sous vide might not sound as intimidating as it did initially. There is no reason why this technique must be limited to professional chefs and fine dining restaurants. Armed with the right knowledge and the right equipment, even an amateur home cook can use this technique efficiently. Once you get the hang of it, it will truly change your relationship with food.

Using sous vide, you can prepare tasty, nutritious, and consistent food every single time. From cooking meat to making desserts, nothing is off-limits. I'm sure you must be quite excited to start trying out different recipes shared in this book. Before you get started, ensure that you have gathered all the ingredients you require, and that you have the necessary cooking equipment. Purchasing the required sous vide tool is a worthy investment that keeps on giving. All you need to do now is select a recipe, follow the instructions, and wait to be pleasantly delighted by the results it produces!

Thank you, and all the best!

REFERENCES

Home, C. 10 benefits of sous vide cooking | Clifton at Home. Retrieved from https://www.cliftonathome.co.uk/sous-vide-cooking/10-benefits-sous-vide-cooking/

Sous Vide Resources | Tips & Tricks | Anova Culinary. Retrieved from https://anovaculinary.com/what-is-sous-vide/sous-vide-resources/

What is Sous Vide? | Everything You Need To Know | Anova Culinary. Retrieved from https://anovaculinary.com/what-is-sous-vide/

USING SOUS VIDE TO COOK WAGYU

John Peters

CHAPTER ONE
ABOUT THE WAGYU BREED

Wagyu is a type of Japanese cattle breed native to Asia. The term Wagyu literally translates to "Japanese cow." These animals were used in agriculture as draft animals and they were chosen because of their physical endurance. These animals were favored because they had more intramuscular fat cells, which provided their body with a readily available source of energy. Wagyu breed has horns, and the cattle are either red or black.

History of the Breed

Research shows that there was some separation in the genes in cattle almost 35,000 years ago, which led to the formation of the Wagyu genetic strain. The Wagyu cattle available today are a result of the crossing of imported breeds with the native cattle in Japan. When the government decided to introduce the Western culture and food habits, Japan imported Brown Swiss, Simmental, Devon, Korean, Ayrshire and Shorthorn cattle. In the year 1910, the infusion of the Asian, British, and European breeds were cut off from outside infusions with other genes.

Four breeds in Japan are considered to have Wagyu strains. These are:

- Japanese Brown, also termed as Red Wagyu in the US
- Japanese Black, the Wagyu breed that is often exported to the US
- Japanese Shorthorn
- Japanese Polled

Japanese Shorthorn or Japanese Polled are not bred in any other parts of the world.

History of the Breed in the US

It was in the year 1975 that Japan first exported the Wagyu breed to the US. Two red and two black bulls were imported to Morris Whitney. The Japanese reduced the tariffs that they imposed on imported beef in the year 1989. This finally encouraged the producers in the US to work on producing a high-quality product for Japan. There were several high qualities of Wagyu imported from Japan to the US in the year 1990. Most of these imported Wagyu were black, and the remainder was red. The producers in the US decided to crossbreed and hence Wagyu had a great influence on the herds here and most other countries across the globe.

Wagyu in the US Today

The American Wagyu Association was set up in Texas in March 1990. This association serves as the registry of the Wagyu cattle in Canada, the US and other countries. The headquarters of this association is in Post Falls. This association promotes and develops a sustainable Wagyu industry in the US. Wagyu beef can offer numerous opportunities. This industry caters to the feeders and breeders. It also targets the high-end restaurants and connects these restaurants with the best producers. The quality of red meat has increased in the US because of the Wagyu breed.

Healthy and Delicious Wagyu Beef

There is no other form of beef that is as tender and tasty as the Wagyu beef. It is for this reason that many gourmet cooks, restaurants and homes across the US seek out and consume Wagyu beef when available. This meat is a gastronomic delight, and it is extremely healthy for you too. The ratio of the saturated to monounsaturated fat is higher in Wagyu when compared to other types of beef. The saturated fat in Wagyu is composed differently as compared to those fats in other types of beef. Stearic acid contains forty percent of the saturated fat in Wagyu beef, but this acid has minimal or no impact on the cholesterol levels in the body, which makes this beef healthier and beneficial to human health.

Wagyu also contains large quantities of conjugated linoleic acid (CLA). This beef has 30% more CLA when compared to other breeds of beef. Foods that have a higher proportion of CLA will have less of a negative effect on health.

Using Sous Vide to Cook Wagyu

Wagyu meat will melt in your mouth if you cook it well. This is also, however, the most expensive kind of beef in the world. So, if you are spending a lot of money on buying the beef, you need to know how to cook it well too. If you are someone who loves to eat Wagyu and are a sous vide enthusiast, you are probably wondering if you can cook Wagyu beef using the sous vide technique.

There are many options: You can cook beef over an open fire either with or without charcoal, straight on a cast iron pan, cook a steak tartare, slice the beef thin or into cubes and cook it, eat it as a 1.5-inch steak or even use the sous vide technique.

Some people are afraid to use this technique to cook Wagyu meat. And you must be wondering if you can? Wouldn't it be better just to sear the meat on a pan? To answer the previous question, yes, you can use the sous vide technique to cook Wagyu. Do you worry because this technique might make the fat melt? Well, it won't. It is important to remember that you can either under or overcook the meat when you sear it on a pan.

The sous vide technique will offer a lot more precision. You can set the temperature to 129 degrees Fahrenheit and know the meat is fully cooked. The fat will be heated and cooked to a texture that will melt in your mouth. You will be sure that the meat is not under or overcooked. So, ignore the chatter about how you should not sous vide Wagyu meat. Be confident that you can reduce your chances of messing up the meat and cook this steak to perfection every time. It is easier to cook Wagyu using the sous vide technique as all you need to do is set the temperature, pop the meat into the machine and watch magic happen as you impress your dinner guests.

CHAPTER TWO
WAGYU RECIPES

Wagyu Sous Vide

Servings: 6 to 8

Ingredients:

- Wagyu fillet
- 1 sprig of rosemary
- Salt to taste
- Pepper to taste

Directions:

1. Take a large pot and place the sous vide in the pot. Pour enough water, so that it crosses the minimum line in the sous vide machine.
2. If you want to cook the meat rare, set the temperature to 120 degrees Fahrenheit. You can look at the other temperatures you can consider at the end of the chapter.
3. Rub the fillet with salt and pepper. Place the fillet in a vacuum-sealed bag. Add the sprig of rosemary to the bag, and seal it.
4. When the temperature in the machine reaches 125 degrees Fahrenheit, drop the bag into the machine.
5. Cook the meat for 45 minutes. It is okay if you forget to pull the meat out in 45 minutes. The temperature of the meat will not exceed the temperature you set in the machine.
6. Place a skillet on medium flame and add olive oil to it. When the Wagyu is done, place the skillet on the pan and cook the meat. Cook on each side for one minute.
7. Cut into slices and serve hot.

Wagyu Steak

Servings: 2 to 6

Ingredients:

- 1 Wagyu steak (1 inch thick)
- 1 clove garlic
- 1 tbsp extra virgin olive oil
- 1 green onion, finely chopped
- 1 tbsp olive oil for searing
- 1 tbsp ponzu
- 2.5 cm daikon radish
- Salt and pepper, as needed

Directions:

1. Place the sous vide machine in a large pot and fill it with water. Make sure to exceed the minimum line inside the machine.
2. Heat the water until it reaches the required temperature. Please review the temperature from the list below.
3. Slice the clove of garlic.
4. While the water heats, remove the excess fat from the Wagyu steak. Rub the steak with salt and pepper. If you are using a vacuum bag, you can place the steak inside the bag. If

you are using a food saver pack, seal one end of the pack.

5. Transfer the steak into the bag and add the slices of garlic. Add a tablespoon of olive oil to the steak. Seal the top of the bag and place it inside the machine.

6. Choose the "moisture" button on the machine.

7. Cook the meat for 60 minutes.

8. While the steak is cooking, grate the daikon and set it aside. Squeeze the daikon and make sure to remove all the liquid.

9. When the steak is done, remove the bag from the machine. Place the steak on a paper towel to remove any extra moisture. You need to do this if you want the steak to have a nice sear.

10. Since the steak was cooked with the garlic, it has a nice aroma and flavor. Remove the garlic slices from the steak. You must remember to never over season the meat since it will absorb the seasoning that you cook it with.

11. Place a pan on medium flame and add oil to it. When the oil is hot, add the steak to the pan and cook it on both sides. You need to cook each side of the steak for at least one minute, so that the steak has a golden-brown crust. If you want a sear mark on the steak, you need to press it down on the map. Do not move the steak in the pan. Flip the steak and repeat the same process. If you want, you can also use a grill to sear the steak.

12. Transfer the steak onto a plate and cut it into slices of ½ an inch. You do not have to worry about letting the meat rest when you use the sous vide technique to cook it.

13. Add a generous amount of grated daikon to the meat and sprinkle the green onion. Pour the ponzu over the steak. If you want, you can serve the steak with some ponzu on the side.

14. If you do not want to eat the meat immediately, you can soak the vacuum bag in ice and then place it in the refrigerator. You can enjoy the meat later.

You can set the temperature in the sous vide machine depending on how you like your meat cooked:

- Rare: 120 degrees Fahrenheit
- Medium rare: 130 degrees Fahrenheit
- Medium: 140 degrees Fahrenheit
- Medium well: 150 degrees Fahrenheit
- Well done: 160 degrees Fahrenheit

Wagyu Brisket with Barbecue Sauce

Servings: 5 to 8

Ingredients:

- 4 pounds Wagyu brisket (preferably Lone Mountain)
- Dry rub (use the ingredients that follow this list)
- tbsp butter, for finishing
- sprigs, for finishing

For the dry rub

- tbsp brown sugar
- tbsp granulated sugar
- 1 ½ tsp chili powder
- tsp garlic powder
- 1 ½ tsp cumin
- 1 ½ tsp paprika
- 1 tsp onion powder
- salt and pepper, to taste

Directions:

1. Place a sous vide machine in a cooking pot and add water to it. Pour the water until the minimum line in the machine.
2. Heat the water to 132 degrees Fahrenheit.
3. While the water heats, combine the ingredients for the dry rub in a bowl and mix them well. You can either rub the entire mixture or store the excess in a container for later.
4. If the brisket is too big, you should slice it into smaller pieces that you can put into the pouch with ease.
5. Rub each piece of the brisket with the seasoning on both sides and put the pieces into a separate vacuum sealed bag. Place the bags in the refrigerator for three hours to let the pieces marinate.
6. Add the sealed pouches to the sous vide machine and cook the meat for 48 hours.

7. Once the pieces are cooked, place a skillet on medium heat. Now, remove the pieces of the brisket from the bags and pat the pieces dry.
8. Place each piece on the pan and cook one side for a minute.
9. Add butter to the pan, and let the meat baste in the butter for a few minutes.
10. Slice the brisket and serve it hot with your favorite sides.

You can set the temperature in the sous vide machine depending on how you like your meat:
- Rare: 120 degrees Fahrenheit
- Medium rare: 130 degrees Fahrenheit
- Medium: 140 degrees Fahrenheit
- Medium well: 150 degrees Fahrenheit
- Well done: 160 degrees Fahrenheit

Made in the USA
Las Vegas, NV
07 February 2022